Home Office Research Study 232

Dalston Youth Project Part II (11 - 14) An Evaluation

Roger Tarling, June Burrows and Alan Clarke

The views expressed in this report are those of the authors, not necessarily those of the Home Office (nor do they reflect Government policy).

Home Office Research, Development and Statistics Directorate
November 2001

Home Office Research Studies

The Home Office Research Studies are reports on research undertaken by or on behalf of the Home Office. They cover the range of subjects for which the Home Secretary has responsibility. Other publications produced by the Research, Development and Statistics Directorate include Findings, Statistical Bulletins and Statistical Papers.

The Research, Development and Statistics Directorate

RDS is also part of the Home Office. The Home Office's purpose is to build a safe, just and tolerant society in which the rights and responsibilities of individuals, families and communities are properly balanced and the protection and security of the public are maintained.

RDS is also part of National Statistics (NS). One of the aims of NS is to inform Parliament and the citizen about the state of the nation and provide a window on the work and performance of government, allowing the impact of government policies and actions to be assessed.

Therefore –

Research Development and Statistics Directorate exists to improve policy making, decision taking and practice in support of the Home Office purpose and aims, to provide the public and Parliament with information necessary for informed debate and to publish information for future use.

First published 2001

Application for reproduction should be made to the Communication Development Unit, Room 201, Home Office, 50 Queen Anne's Gate, London SW1H 9AT.
© Crown copyright 2001   ISBN 1 84082 768.8
                                    ISSN 0072 6435

Foreword

This paper is one of a group of development reports about projects funded by the Home Office Programme Development Unit (PDU), part of the Research Development and Statistics Directorate. The PDU existed from 1992 to 2000; it was set up specifically to encourage, fund and develop innovative local projects about issues related to crime and criminal justice. Its objective was to try to build a bridge between pure research and practice. Two cycles of funding were made available: 1992-1995 and 1996-1999.

Evaluation reports of the five projects funded in the second phase, including this one, are being published in the Home Office Research Study series. Also being published to coincide with these reports are a small number of evaluation reports from the first phase of work, which involved extremely experimental approaches both to development and to evaluation. These are being published as Occasional Papers.

All of these reports relate to early intervention initiatives directed at providing support to children who are, as a rule, not offenders but whose lives include a number of the circumstances which have been identified as risk factors for offending. Interventions include work with young primary school pupils and first-time offenders and, as in this report, with young people who may be experiencing social exclusion as a result of particular circumstances.

The PDU programme was extremely developmental, and evaluators were specifically tasked not only to consider the outcomes of the projects (which in many cases, because of the nature of the interventions and the ages of the participants, can only be early or intermediate outcomes in any case) but also to look carefully at the process of development and implementation and to include a substantial core of descriptive material about the participants and their circumstances. The reports provide a great deal of useful material about the characteristics of the young people involved and their families. They also describe the ways in which agencies responsible for interventions relate to their clients and to each other, discuss the practicality and success of interventions themselves and analyse early indicators of success or failure. All of this knowledge is especially relevant to the many new initiatives either under way or planned, including the Children and Young Persons' Unit programmes and New Deal for Communities, together with much other national and local crime reduction work. Although the degree of evaluative rigour varies, these reports nonetheless contain valuable and constructive learning about why, for whom and how intervention should be planned.

This report on the Dalston Youth Project II (DYP II) describes an innovative approach to working with children aged 11 – 14 and at risk of being excluded from school, by offering a combination of mentoring support and supplementary education.

Mentoring is increasingly frequently used to support young people in a variety of contexts. The evaluators' report carefully documents the way in which mentoring was conceived and organised for this project and describes the nature of the mentoring relationship. There are both parallels and differences between the structure and processes described here and those outlined in the report on Project CHANCE, which also offered mentoring support but to much younger children. In both cases, the evaluators note the importance of providing continuing support, training and backup for mentors throughout the life of the relationship.

The evaluators also record the problems of sustaining the mentor-mentee relationship; this was a particularly difficult area for DYP II – less so for the younger age group in Project CHANCE – and points to the need to consider the developmental stage of mentees very carefully when planning a mentoring programme.

DYP II achieved some clear successes. A number of children made modest progress towards improved behaviour and attitudes to learning; and for a smaller group, there were major and significant changes. Maintaining the commitment of young people, who were often experiencing multiple problems, to a programme which demanded a great deal of time and effort was challenging. Success was clearly related to the extent of participation.

Here, the evaluators raise another question which is relevant to many intervention and support programmes. The criteria which DYP II applied were rigorous in that young people were not enrolled on the programme unless they were experiencing serious problems and had multiple needs. This in itself meant that 'success' was unlikely to be achieved by everyone. Should programmes focus on the most 'at risk' group and accept that failure to achieve objectives will be more likely, or should interventions concentrate on young people where problems and needs are not yet so severe and for whom intervention might be more effective?

The evaluators also note that some of the successful young people were also receiving support from other intervention programmes and question whether single and time-limited interventions are worthwhile.

The report contains valuable lessons for development, project managers and practitioners.

Christine Lehman RDS

1   St James-Roberts & Singh (2001) Can mentors help primary school children with behaviour problems? HORS 233, London, Home Office

Contents

Executive summary

Research has consistently shown that young people are at risk of offending if they come from unstable family backgrounds, have poor relationships with their parents, receive inadequate parental supervision and have delinquent siblings and peers. Delinquent behaviour may be precipitated by, and go hand-in-hand with, poor performance at school. as indicated by truancy and lack of engagement at school, disruptive behaviour and low levels of achievement.

The Dalston Youth Project (DYPII) is located within the London Borough of Hackney, which is one of the most deprived inner city areas in the country. The project was conceived to work with young people aged between 11 and 14 who were defined to be 'at risk' of dropping out of school and of becoming involved in offending behaviour. It planned to offer them some support during the formative period of early adolescence and to direct them towards a more socially acceptable and safer lifestyle. There were four main strands to the programme:

- *residential weekend;*

- *mentoring component;*

- *educational component;* and

- *parent/guardian component.*

The project's four aims and objectives were defined as:

1. to improve basic education skills (literacy, numeracy, life skills) in the target group as well as to increase the group's motivation to learn;

2. to improve social skills and reduce conflict with parents and other adults;

3. to reduce offending rates, drug use, truanting or other at-risk behaviour within the target group; and

4. to establish a team of volunteers in the local community trained and supported by the project to act as mentors to the young people.

Selection of young people

It was envisaged that a cohort of 30 young people (20 boys and 10 girls) would participate each year. Thus at the end of the third year, it was hoped that a total of 90 young people would have participated in the project. Referrals were taken from three local schools that had significant numbers of pupils from disadvantaged backgrounds and pupils for whom English was a second language. Criteria for referral were designed to identify those young people most in need of intervention. Those referred were generally underachieving at school and their lack of educational attainment went hand-in-hand with behavioural problems. Most of the young people came from materially poor home backgrounds, living in dysfunctional families.

In the first and second years, 26 young people joined DYP and in the third year, 28 joined. This made a total of 80, ten short of the original target.

residential weekend

The residential weekend, set in an activity centre, was the formal start of the project and was deemed to be a great success. Its focus was to engage and identify young people and mentors with the project and the demanding activities were intended to build confidence and raise self-esteem. In addition, the weekend was an opportunity to assess in greater detail, the suitability of mentors and introduce them to the young people.

Mentoring component

As far as youth crime is concerned, it has been suggested that adult mentors can offer young people from unstable family backgrounds an alternative source of practical help, emotional support, guidance and care, as well as provide them with positive role models. Mentoring formed one of the key components of DYP II and the development of a successful mentoring relationship was an integral feature of the overall programme.

A little over 70 per cent of mentors were female. The majority were aged between 20 and 35 and from minority ethnic backgrounds. Over three-quarters were in full-time employment and the vast majority had been involved in some form of voluntary work in the past.

Motivations for becoming a mentor were primarily focused around wanting to help disadvantaged young people. In some cases it was not only a wish to do something 'useful' but a desire to try and help someone overcome the kinds of problems and difficulties the mentors themselves had experienced in their own teenage years. Many also saw mentoring as important in terms of their own personal development.

The initial training and induction of the mentors took place over two weekends, prior to the residential weekend. It provided a broad introduction to the fundamental aspects of mentoring and gave participants a general feel for some of the main issues surrounding working with young people. A programme of regular training sessions was implemented and mentors had the option to take an accredited course; 20 chose to do so. Mentors were able to discuss any problems they had on an informal basis with project staff and they were also encouraged to attend the mentor support evenings.

Project staff took into account the pair's interests when matching mentors and mentees. Pairings were observed at the residential weekend, where the activities were constructed so as to bring each potential mentor-mentee pairing together. If a good relationship did not appear to be developing then there was time during the weekend to test out alternative pairings.

The mentoring relationship

A number of mentors experienced difficulties at the outset in establishing a relationship and in identifying the scope of the mentoring role. With the introduction of mentor support evenings, these initial concerns about the boundaries of the mentoring role were addressed. While mentors saw themselves as befriending a young person in difficult circumstances, thus providing mentees with an opportunity to discuss their problems with someone who did not constitute an authority figure, they also considered themselves to have a significant part to play in helping young people to improve their self-esteem. Mentors stressed the importance of not being overtly judgmental at the outset of a relationship, but of listening to the young person and gradually winning his or her trust and confidence. Although they recognised the importance of finding something that their mentees were good at and then giving them praise and encouragement, they also saw it as part of their responsibility to question and challenge inappropriate behaviour. In addition, they were conscious of the need to encourage their mentees to take decisions and set themselves achievable goals. However, the mentoring relationship was very much a reciprocal relationship that benefited both parties.

When asked what a mentor was, none of the young people who were interviewed had any difficulty in describing the role and functions of a mentor. For example, one young person said:

> A mentor is your own personal person. You can talk to that person and they won't tell anybody else. They are like a second sister or brother. A really, really good friend. They help you with your education.

It was found that about a half of the mentor-mentee matches were successful in that they maintained contact throughout the 12 months of the project.

Educational component

As a primary aim of the project was to re-motivate those on the verge of dropping out of mainstream schooling and to improve their basic education skills, the educational component was a key aspect of the project. The educational component evolved and adapted as a result of the experience gained by the project, the changing needs of the young people and in response to staff turnover and other logistical and practical issues.

The plan of the project was to provide each young person with six hours of tuition after school, each week during term time. The turnover of tutors proved to be a particular problem. During the three-year period, nine tutors were engaged by the project and this inevitably caused disruption to the planning and delivery of the education component.

After-school classes

At the outset it was recognised that in order to engage disaffected young people the education component had to be different from mainstream schooling. If it was too formal it would be seen as no different from mainstream school and the young people would stay away. On the other hand, DYP II was not to be a youth club. In addition, the education component placed an emphasis on rewarding achievement and building up self-esteem.

The tutors were asked what particular problems the young people posed and why they thought those on the project had not been succeeding in mainstream school. The tutors felt that the problems were more of a personal than an educational nature. Starting with disadvantages, the young people had fallen behind. An inevitable cycle of decline then took hold. They became aggressive and disruptive to cover up their failings. They then formed peer groups which reinforced that it was not 'cool' to conform or succeed at school.

The classes were thus a mixture of activities. Young people would spend some time writing in their diaries (which became an important vehicle for self expression and communication with staff) or preparing work for presentation evenings. They would watch a video or read abstracts from a book selected to raise particular issues which could then form the subject of discussion. Much of the discussion would be about appropriate behaviours and the development of social skills. The young people might plan trips or write 'thank you' letters or reports following a trip. Much of the work would be undertaken on computer. It was felt important to identify topics and materials that would engage the young people and to let them have a say in the planning of the class.

Outwardly and collectively the young people were dismissive of education and they felt that their school had a negative view of them. However, privately and individually the young people confessed to not being able to read, write or 'do maths'. This embarrassed them and as a consequence they had low self-esteem. Much work early in the project year was spent addressing behavioural problems and in 'settling' the young people in order that they could function as a class. They had to be taught how to learn and be given confidence to achieve. Those who did attend classes regularly said that they enjoyed the classes and were benefiting from them.

Some classes ran smoothly but others were interrupted by inappropriate behaviour. While attempts were made to redeem the situation by discussion and negotiation, sometimes discipline had to be enforced and young people sent home.

In the first two years a little under a half of the young people regularly attended classes. Not only was there a significant variation in attendance between young people but attendance declined over time and there was a steep decline after each holiday break. In Year 3 letters were written to each young person welcoming them back and tutors visited them and their parents in their homes in preparation for the new term. Attendance improved in Year 3 and was more consistent throughout the year – 17 of the 28 young people attended more than 50 per cent of their classes.

Parenting component

Despite early efforts, this strand of the project turned out to be the most difficult to organise and the least successful. The project had aimed to involve parents/guardians, to provide twice-monthly parenting skills sessions and to make home visits in order to undertake family counselling where appropriate. It appeared that most parents saw the project as being for the young people, not for them, and they tended not to participate in the sessions that were designed to develop their own parenting skills. They did, however, support their child by attending presentation evenings and graduation night. And project staff were able to provide much needed support to several individual parents at times of extreme difficulty.

Graduation Night

The project formally ended with Graduation Night at which young people and mentors received certificates of commendation for their efforts and performance throughout the year. Each Graduation Night was fully supported by parents, family and friends.

Impact of the project

A simple measure for assessing impact was to look at the number of young people graduating from the project each year who received a certificate of commendation in acknowledgement of their efforts. Approximately two-thirds of young people graduated in Years 1 and 2 and a higher proportion, about three-quarters, graduated in Year 3. However, as the project naturally wanted to make formal acknowledgement of any effort wherever it was able to do so, the number graduating overstates the success of the project.

In years 2 and 3 specific achievements were cited on the certificate and this provided a more detailed assessment of the impact of the project. Looking at the citations on the certificates and cross-checking these with project staff and school representatives, it was found that between 10 and 12 young people had improved their behaviour, self-esteem and academic competencies. Formal verification of improvements in educational attainment was possible in Year 3 when the project administered reading and mathematics tests. The results were not spectacular and the project tutors did not claim them to be.

Progress at DYP II was not always matched by progress at school. Only a small number showed improvements in school attendance, school work or behaviour at school.

Longer-term outcomes

At the end of Year 3 schools were asked to assess the subsequent progress of those 52 young people who had been included in the project in the first two years. Twelve young people could not be followed up. Of the 40 remaining young people, 19 were adjudged to have been a success and 21 a failure. In order to assess whether the project had contributed to a young person's success the group was divided according to whether they had participated in the project. In the first instance participation was taken to be that the young person had been a regular and committed attendee of the educational classes. Those who took full part in the educational classes at the project were found to be much more likely to be a success in the longer term. A full 87 per cent of those who participated in the educational classes were judged to have been a success compared with only 24 per cent of those who did not participate. This relationship was found to be statistically significant. Although encouraging, it should be remembered that those not attending the project are not a true control group but merely those who were initially selected but chose not to continue after the early stages. Thus the results may simply reflect a 'selection effect' – that is, those who continued with the project were the better prospects of success regardless of the achievements of the project.

A similar analysis was undertaken for the mentoring component of the project. This time young people were differentiated according to whether they had a good relationship with their mentor. Those having a mentor were more likely to be successful in the longer term. However, this association was not so marked and did not attain statistical significance.

Offending behaviour

The final criterion on which the project could be assessed was its aim to reduce the risk of offending. Information on offending was provided by the police for each of the 80 young people on the project. Of these, 32 (40%) were cautioned or convicted of an offence at some stage. There was a difference between boys and girls; only three of the 26 girls (12%) committed offences compared with 29 of the 54 boys (54%). The young people committed a wide variety of offences before, during and after being on the project. The majority were property offences but there were also some serious crimes against the person. About one-half of the young people who had committed offences had only committed one offence. At the other extreme, two young people had committed six offences and one, seven offences.

Conclusions

The project exists to help 'at risk' young people, and by all accounts those participating in the project during the three years were a challenging group. The project did achieve some level of success with about half the young people (and considerable success with five or six of them). But half did not engage with the project in any meaningful way. This raises two issues. First, were the right young people referred to the project? Second, is a one-year project long enough to consolidate the gains made and enable those who do participate to make further progress?

Introduction

Research has consistently shown over a long period of time that young people are at risk of offending if they come from unstable family backgrounds, have poor relationships with their parents, receive inadequate parental supervision and have delinquent siblings and peers. Delinquent behaviour may be precipitated by, and go hand-in-hand with, poor performance at school, as indicated by lack of engagement at school and truancy, disruptive behaviour and low levels of achievement (Tarling, 1993; Graham and Bowling, 1995; Audit Commission, 1996; Farrington, 1996).

Research and statistics also reveal that the peak age of offending for both males and females is during the mid-to late-teen years (Tarling, 1993). Thus the period between ages 11 and 14 is often crucial in a young person's life and can have a major bearing on whether he or she succeeds in mainstream schooling, drops out or becomes involved in drug misuse and offending behaviour.

The Dalston Youth Project (DYP II) was conceived to work with the age group of young people (11 – 14) who were defined to be 'at risk' (by showing signs of deviant behaviour). It planned to offer them some support during the formative period of early adolescence. The intervention provided by the project would, it was hoped, reorientate them back towards a more socially acceptable and safe lifestyle.

The DYP programme contained four main components.

1. *residential weekend.* This was held at a dedicated outdoor activity centre and the two days served to get the project off to a memorable start. It enabled relationships to be formed and led participants to identify with and show commitment to the project.

2. *mentoring component.* The young people were matched with a volunteer from the local community, who was trained to support them as they began to achieve academically and socially.

3. *educational component.* The young people participated in an intensive educational support programme designed to improve their basic education skills as well as their motivation to learn.

4. *parent/guardian component*. Parents were offered opportunities to develop their own parenting skills and were given advice on how to support their child's participation in the project.

Although distinct, the four components were seen to be inter-linked and mutually supportive. Tutors, mentors and parents all interacted in various ways to reinforce and help deliver the project's aims and objectives, which were defined as:

1. to improve basic education skills (literacy, numeracy, life skills) in the target group as well as to increase the group's motivation to learn;

2. to improve social skills and reduce conflict with parents and other adults;

3. to reduce offending rates, drug use, truanting or other at-risk behaviour within the target group; and

4. to establish a team of volunteers in the local community trained and supported by the project to act as mentors to the young people.

It can be seen then that DYP II set out to address the specific factors that make young people more vulnerable. It aimed to rectify deficiencies in home background by offering parental support, to compensate for dysfunctional families and lack of parental support by providing an additional responsible adult in the young person's life and to tackle the problems that the young person was experiencing at school.

The initial plan stated that 30 young people would be selected to participate in the project. The project would last for one year and would be repeated in Years 2 and3 (and each year thereafter) with a new cohort of young people. DYP II received Home Office Development Fund money from September 1996 to cover the costs of the first three years. The infrastructure for some parts of the project was already in place. DYP had, for three years prior to this project, been running a mentoring programme for older (15-18 year-old) young people (DYP I) but this older programme did not include after school classes. This element was new to the younger project (DYP II) and had to be developed. DYP II also included a more ambitious parenting programme.

The project cycle began with the recruitment of mentors in October – their initial training took place early in the New Year. Young people were referred to the project and the agreement of those selected was secured in time for all to attend the residential weekend in late February. A Graduation Night was held in December and marked the formal end of the project. Years 2 and 3 followed a similar pattern and timetable, although in Year 3 the project cycle ran approximately two months later.

Home Office funding amounted to approximately £90,000 per year and was sufficient to meet the costs of a project director and three part-time tutors, the costs of the residential weekend, some further trips and activities, mentors' expenses and the costs of learning resources. (Half way through the three year period, a part-time mentor support post was created.) The cost of additional staff and resources, in particular the DYP Director post and an administrator together with the premises, were shared with DYP I so the Home Office grant met only a part of these costs. The full cost of the project was estimated to be £110,000 per year. Looked at another way, if the full complement of 30 young people participated in the project, the cost per young person was approximately £3,700 per annum.

Selection of young people

The original documentation stated that young people would be recruited from a variety of sources. Project staff would make presentations to teams of Hackney probation officers, social workers, education welfare workers, teachers, police officers, youth workers and others. It was envisaged that young people could also refer themselves or be referred by parents or friends. In the event it was decided early on by the steering committee to work with a limited number of nearby schools and accept referrals from only those schools. This seemed a sensible and pragmatic approach enabling the project to work closely with the schools, in terms of receiving assistance and information from schools and in providing feedback to them on the needs and progress of the young people. Restricting the number of schools reduced the number of contacts that had to be made, and because the they were located geographically close to the project, the young people did not have far to travel.

In the first two years the project worked with two nearby secondary schools: a boys' school and a girls' school. They were selected not only on the basis of their geographical location but also on their level of need. As boys are more likely to be 'at risk' than girls, (that is more likely to be excluded and more likely to offend), the steering committee decided to recruit twice as many boys (20 per cohort) than girls (10 per cohort) to the project. Although the project was initially conceived for 11 to 14 year-olds it was agreed that the schools would not have sufficient information to make informed decisions on 11 year-olds who were in their first year of the secondary school. Thus it was decided that 10 boys from Year 8 (12 to 13 year-olds) and 10 boys from Year 9 (13 to 14 year-olds) would be selected from the boys school and 10 girls from Year 8 from the girls' school. (Note that as the project ran for a calendar year, the Year 8 young people were in Year 9 when they left the project and those in Year 9 at the outset completed the project while in Year 10.)

In the third year, a further, mixed, school was invited to work with the project. This school was allocated 10 places and the quota for the boys' school was reduced from 20 to 10. Although the mixed school could refer boys and girls it chose to refer only boys, all from Year 8. The boys' school decided not to refer any more Year 9 boys. Thus the composition of the third cohort consisted of two groups of boys and one group of girls all drawn from Year 8. The groups were drawn from a boys' school, a girls' school and a mixed school.

The schools

Throughout this report the schools will be named and referred to as 'Boys School', Girls School' and 'Mixed School'.

All three schools faced a demanding task. All had significant numbers of pupils from ethnic minority backgrounds and pupils for whom English was a second language. Boys School pointed out that over 30 different languages were represented in the school. Pupils came from disadvantaged backgrounds; one indicator of this was that 90 per cent qualified for free school meals. The student population was very mobile. Just before the start of this project Boys School had to absorb a large intake of students following the closure of another Hackney school. Much of the energy of Boys School was absorbed in applying (as it subsequently turned out, successfully) for technology college status.

Girls School devoted considerable effort during the three years to its campaign to remain an all-girls-school. During the period the schools were the subject of Ofsted inspections.

In addition, the education system in Hackney was the subject of extensive debate, attention and reorganisation. Not surprisingly, all the schools felt somewhat beleaguered with a substantial number of different problems to occupy their time and resources. These other problems influenced the commitment the schools could devote to DYP at various points throughout the three-year period. It should also be pointed out that the schools were involved in other experimental programmes and initiatives, and some of the young people selected for DYP II were also the subjects of other programmes.

The wider context

The project is located within the London Borough of Hackney, which is one of the most deprived inner city areas in the country. An audit profiling poverty in Hackney carried out shortly before the project began (Griffiths, 1996) documented the extent of deprivation in the area. The borough had responded by drawing up plans and in devising initiatives. DYP II featured in the Hackney Children's Plan, the borough's comprehensive plan of services and provisions for children and families. The chair of the Children's Plan Steering Group and head of social services, said that the borough was keen to work with imaginative or innovative independent projects. DYP II fitted well within that portfolio. It was important for the borough to know whether a project which provided volunteers and a fresh start for the young people (as offered by DYP II) could successfully work with families that had become unresponsive to, and suspicious of, all statutory agencies such as the police, social services and education. The chair pointed out that the average cost to the borough of placing one young person in residential care was £3,000 per week. On that basis the project would break even if it only achieved one person staying out of residential care for seven or eight months. However, he pointed out that DYP II was but one experimental project within the borough.

The steering committee
Direct and tangible support for DYP II came in the appointment of a member of the Childrens Plan Group to chair the steering committee. Other local agencies were represented on the committee including the Education Welfare Service, the Pupil Referral Unit and the Youth Service. When interviewed, representatives of these agencies emphasised the value that they placed on innovative projects such as DYP II in providing an alternative and fresh approach to dealing with challenging young people. They pointed out that the statutory nature and role of their own agency restricted the options available to them.

Also represented on the steering committee were the schools (two initially and later three), the Youth and Community Department of the local police, the Home Office (funders of the project), Crime Concern, the evaluators and project staff (in particular the project co-ordinator and the mentor co-ordinator).

The steering committee met on 27 occasions during the three-and-a-half-year period which included the initial design and start-up phase and three cohorts of young people. Thus the steering committee met approximately every six to seven weeks and provided a significant input into the planning and subsequent development of the project. It assessed every aspect of the project from broad structural questions and strategy to detailed issues such as the policy on discipline and grievance procedures. In the later stages of the project it also discussed fund raising. In addition to meeting formally as a committee, members also contributed their specialist knowledge to specific issues as they arose. Committee members also sat on recruitment boards and panels.

The commitment and the constructive contribution that members gave, together with the continuity provided by the steering committee, undoubtedly assisted the project. The Committee was an example of harmonious multi-agency co-operation. There were no inter-agency jealousies or rivalries, and as a result project staff felt able to share issues and concerns honestly and openly. Staff valued this opportunity as it enabled them to draw on the advice and expertise of the committee and to feel more confident in the decisions reached. Each year members of the steering committee, together with tutors and some mentors, spent an 'awayday' reviewing the achievements and disappointments of the previous year and revising the plan for the year ahead. These gatherings too were informative, supportive and constructive and formed an extremely productive part of the project development process. The role of the steering committee in maintaining continuity, in offering guidance and support and in providing a vehicle for sharing and challenging ideas across agencies, cannot be overestimated.

Evaluation methodology

From the outset, a dual-purpose evaluation research design strategy was adopted focusing on both formative and summative issues (Clarke, 1999). On a formative level the emphasis was on exploring how the intervention programme offered by DYP II was conceptualised, organised and implemented. In the early phase of the research the primary objective was to describe the content and structure of the programme and to   investigate the experiences of the different groups of people involved. This involved a multi-method approach to data collection, which included:

- a review of the literature produced by DYP II describing the programme;

- attendance at Steering Committee meetings and 'awaydays';

- semi-structured interviews with members of DYP II staff;

- non-participant observation at the residential weekend, mentor training sessions and other activities organised by the project;

- classroom observations of the educational classes;

- semi-structured interviews and conversations with young people, mentors, and parents/guardians;

- site visits to the participating schools; and

- extraction of information from DYP II and school records.

The idea was that the qualitative data generated in this way would provide an insight into how well the major components were implemented and how they were received by programme participants. In addition to examining general implementation issues, the formative evaluation monitored the administrative arrangements and mechanisms that were in place as part of the routine management of the project. The intention was that this information would help to uncover strengths and weaknesses in the design and implementation of the various components and thereby help project staff to decide what changes needed to be made to the programme.

While conducting the formative evaluation it was possible to begin to explore ways in which a summative evaluation might be mounted. From a methodological point of view, when conducting an outcome evaluation it is advantageous to have a control or comparison group against which to compare the group subjected to the intervention. This increases the degree to which any observed differences can be attributed to the impact of the intervention. Consequently, the evaluators spent a considerable amount of time in the early stages of the research exploring the possibility of obtaining a control group of young people, matched to those young people on the project in terms of educational ability, standards of behaviour and the like. Unfortunately, there were a number of practical difficulties that made it impossible to mount a controlled study. For example, a control group could not be drawn from the same schools that provided young people for the project. This is because those who were selected to attend DYP II were chosen precisely because they met strict criteria in terms of irregular attendance, disruptive behaviour and poor literacy skills. Therefore, any other pupils chosen from within the feeder schools would not constitute a satisfactory control group because they would not have a similar profile and could be expected to fare better than the DYP II group even though they had not been subject to any intervention. Consideration was given to identifying a control within other schools in Hackney, but professionals within the Local Education Department advised that there were no comparable schools which could yield an appropriate cohort of young people. Furthermore, it was pointed out that it would be especially difficult to enlist the co-operation of other schools when there was no incentive for them to participate, as they did not receive any direct benefit from the project. Given these practical difficulties it was not possible to adopt a quasi-experimental evaluation research design. However, retrospectively, it did prove possible to undertake some limited comparisons between those who participated in the project and those who dropped out at an early stage.

In measuring outcomes a mixture of qualitative and quantitative indicators were employed. These included the number of young people successfully completing the mentoring and educational components of the project. Reading and mathematics tests were administered and evidence of involvement in criminal activity was available from police records. Professional assessments were obtained from tutors and school representatives, and perceptions and experiences were obtained from all those involved, in particular the mentors and the young people themselves.

A longitudinal or 'follow up' element was built into the research design in order that some assessment could be made of the longer term impact of the project. At the end of the three years an assessment was undertaken of the subsequent progress of all young people passing through the programme. This meant that the young people in the first cohort were assessed two years after their participation in the project. Members of the second cohort were assessed one year after their participation in the project, but no follow -up was possible for the third and final cohort.

During the course of the three years, the evaluators:

- attended 21 of the 27 steering committee meetings (three of these were held before the evaluators were appointed);

- attended two residential weekends;

- attended three mentor training days;

- attended three mentor support evenings;

- attended four presentation evenings;

- attended all three awaydays;

- attended all three Graduation Nights;

- observed 28 after-school education classes;

- formally interviewed project staff on two occasions per year;

- interviewed 43 young people (many more than once);

- interviewed eight mentors;

- interviewed three parents in their homes;

- interviewed all members of the steering committee;

- interviewed school representatives on eight occasions.

The above records the formal and planned interviews and observations, but on other occasions, as and when the opportunity arose, the evaluators spoke to project staff, young people, mentors and all those connected with the project. For example, when observing a class there were opportunities before and after to speak to young people and tutors and discussions were held with all mentors who attended mentor support evenings. Even social events, such as the Quiz Night organised to raise funds for the project, provided an opportunity to discuss aspects of the project informally.

In addition, all documentation was examined which recorded the activities of the project and details of the young people and mentors. Information on offending was obtained from the police. The schools also provided information on each young person's participation in schooling and on their educational attainment. Further information was gathered from completed tests and questionnaires.

2   The young people

Young people could only be selected for the programme if they met the specific criteria set by project staff and the steering committee. Young people referred had to meet five of the following seven attributes:

1. *Poor school attendance*
- lower than 90 per cent and
- lowest 20 per cent of year group

2. *Special Educational Needs (SEN)*
- any stage of the SEN profile system and
- concerns of emotional behavioural difficulties (EBD)

3. *Frequent removal from lessons for disruptive behaviour*
- frequent removal from class and
- highest 20 per cent of year group

4. *Low level of literacy*
- lowest 20 per cent of year group

5. *Current concern to other agencies*
- (for example: youth justice, social services, education psychology and police)

6. *Disciplinary*
- above average involvement in the school's disciplinary procedure

7. *Teacher judgement*
Considered probable (over 70% chance) by year head that one of the following would occur if there was no intervention:
- young person would leave school before completing GCSEs;
- permanent exclusion;
- a number of fixed-term exclusions.

These criteria were designed to identify the young people most in need of intervention. In the event, they proved to be too restrictive and were relaxed somewhat in later years (it was no longer a requirement that a young person had to meet five criteria). Even so, despite more flexibility no cohort attained the planned allocation of 30. The numbers joining the project from each school and in each cohort are set out in Table 1.

Table 1: Number of young people joining the project by school and cohort

| | Boys School | | Girls School | Mixed School | Total |
	Year 8	Year 9	Year 8	Year 8	
Cohort 1	8	10	8	-	26
Cohort 2	10	7	9	-	26
Cohort 3	9	-	9	10	28
Total	27	17	26	10	80

The ethnic composition of each cohort is given in Table 2.

Table 2: Ethnic background of the young people joining the project

	Cohort 1	Cohort 2	Cohort 3	Total
White	6	10	6	22
African	6	6	6	18
Caribbean	11	7	12	30
Turkish	1	1	-	2
Asian	1	-	1	2
Other (mixed race)	1	2	3	6
Total	26	26	28	80

It can be seen that nearly three-quarters of the young people came from ethnic minority backgrounds. There was little difference between the cohorts; all three comprised a majority from minority ethnic groups. There was little difference between schools in the backgrounds of people referred, except that Girls School was slightly more likely to refer girls from African backgrounds; 10 of the 18 from such a background were girls.

Given the criteria that had to be met to be eligible for the project, the young people referred were, by definition, underachieving at school. Their lack of educational attainment went hand-in-hand with behavioural problems. The young people's reading ages (where they were recorded) were invariably three years, and sometimes five years, below their chronological age. Interestingly, five young people had absented themselves from school on every occasion the tests were administered. It was felt that this action was taken in order to conceal their inadequacies and to avoid embarrassment to themselves. Not all the young people referred to the project were experiencing educational difficulties: nine young people were recorded as being 'of average intelligence' and three of them 'bright'. However, despite their ability, they were 'not engaging with lessons'. Of the 80 young people, 39 had been referred to Education Welfare Services and the vast majority (69) were at some stage of the SEN profile system. Furthermore, seven had been referred to an educational psychologist and four had spent some time at the special Pupil Referral Unit (PRU). Four had been provided with home school support or a school counsellor.

The behavioural problems identified included, tantrums, rudeness and challenging authority, persistent low-level-disruption, swearing, aggressive behaviour including threats, bullying and fighting. Some behaviour was attributable to emotional difficulties or the need to 'seek attention'. The young people's behaviour frequently resulted in breaches of the schools' disciplinary codes and 47 had received at least one fixed-term exclusion. Most of these had received more than one (although because of the way the data was recorded, some fixed term exclusions may have occurred after the young person was referred to DYP II).

Most young people came from materially poor home backgrounds, and were living in dysfunctional families. Detailed information on home circumstances was available for 63 young people. Only 13 of them were living with both natural parents. No less than 43 were living in single parent households, 35 with their mother and eight with their father. In seven of these 43 households the parent was living with a partner. Of the remaining seven young people, two were living with their grandparents, four with an aunt and one was living with foster parents. Some were living in large families where the single parent had difficulty managing, but several lived alone with a single parent who appeared to take little interest in the young person's upbringing.

Further indication of the difficulties these families were facing could be gauged by the extent of their involvement with other agencies. Nineteen were 'known' to social services and two of the young people were on the 'at risk' register. Five were being assisted by the Child and Family Consultation Service or by a child guidance counsellor. Two parents (one young person's mother and another's father) were in prison).

There were early signs that the young people were beginning to become involved in crime. Eight of the 80 (10%) had each been cautioned or convicted for one offence. The offences included shoplifting (two young people), criminal damage (one young person), motor vehicle offences (two), assault (one) and robbery (two).

In discussion with schools, mentors and the young people themselves, it was clear that these young people did not have home backgrounds conducive or supportive of succeeding at school or in other aspects of life. One school representative said "there is little at home for these students". As a result most young people seemed to lack self-esteem.

When asked why they had referred the young person to the project, the school representative would often state that it was to compensate for poor home circumstances and to give the young person new experiences through attending the residential or the other trips arranged by the project. The mentoring component was seen to be important to provide, often for the first time, a responsible adult who might act as an alternative role model for the young person. By taking an interest in the young person it was felt that the mentor could open up new horizons and help the young person develop new interests. The educational classes were seen as a less formal or 'authoritarian' setting than mainstream school which might help to stimulate an interest in learning and re-engage the young person in a way that the school could not.

3   Residential weekend

The residential component marked the formal start of the project and on each occasion took place over one weekend (from Friday evening until Sunday afternoon) in the spring at Hindleap Warren, in East Sussex. Hindleap Warren is a dedicated activity centre run by professionally qualified staff who devise the programme, supervise the activities and take care of all arrangements. Hiring this kind of facility ensured that the weekend was well organised to the benefit and enjoyment of the young people and mentors taking part as well as the project staff.

As a dramatic and memorable start to the project, the residential weekend served four purposes:

- it engaged and identified young people and mentors with the project;

- it provided an opportunity to further assess the suitability of mentors;

- it provided an informal setting to introduce to each other mentors and young people who were meeting for the first time; and

- it built confidence and raised self-esteem by providing a demanding schedule of physical activities.

On all four counts the weekend fully served its purposes. The young people were split into small groups and undertook each of the challenging activities in rotation. Mentors were allocated to each group. There was a sense of excitement and comradeship which heightened positive feelings towards the project. The sense of achievement was apparent from those who had successfully completed the challenging activities – such as walking across a narrow beam 60 feet above ground level or successfully negotiating a labyrinth of underground narrow tunnels. Everyone appeared to enjoy themselves and many relationships were formed.

As the programme was run by the staff at the centre, DYP II staff were freed from administration and could spend the time getting to know the young people and mentors (who were meeting for the first time) and facilitating the development of relationships. They could also observe the interaction of young people and mentors. Their observations, together with the information staff obtained about each person's personality and interests (and in the case of mentors their experience), was used to make final decisions on pairings. It was also an opportunity to identify those thought not suitable to be mentors. (For example, In Year 2, one person was judged not to be suitable and was omitted from further involvement with the project.)

It was clear from being present at the weekend that the residential component worked well in many respects. The weekend encouraged a good atmosphere and everyone took part in a positive spirit. The activities were well organised and groups were focussed on the task at hand. Also noticeable was the level of encouragement and support each member of a group gave to the other members. The observations of DYP II staff were insightful and the matching of young person and mentor was thoughtful and well done. The weekend also served its purpose of enabling staff, young people and mentors to get to know each other better and to become positively associated with the project.

Attendance at the three residential weekends is given in the table below.

Table 3: Number of young people and mentors attending the Residential Weekend

	Young People	Mentors
Year 1	23	28
Year 2	17	27
Year 3	21	22

Compared with Year 1, the success of the residential weekend in Year 2 suffered a little as a result of the delay in referring young people to the project. Because of the delays only 17 young people (11 boys and 6 girls) attended. This meant that nine people who joined the project later did not benefit from the experience. Furthermore, it resulted in an imbalance between mentors and young people. At the end of the weekend, when everyone was gathered in the main hall, the project co-ordinator publicly announced the young person and mentor pairings. Although the co-ordinator said that future pairings would take place once more young people joined the project, it did not alleviate the feeling of rejection experienced by ten mentors whose names had not been called out. The embarrassment was quickly recognised by project staff who resolved to arrange things differently next year. (In Year 3 pairings did not take place at the residential weekend but at a special 'games' evening which took place a week later.)

4   Mentoring Component

Although mentoring is currently in vogue the idea has been around for some considerable time. The term 'mentor' has its roots in Greek mythology, where it appears in Homer's *Odyssey*. Mentor was the name of the trusted son of Alimus, who was chosen by Odysseus to act as a guardian, teacher and adviser to his son Telemachus. As Dondero notes, 'The word "mentor" has since come to mean a loyal, wise and trusted teacher and friend' (1997: 881). The actual process of mentoring, referred to as mentorship, has been described as 'a close interpersonal "helping relationship" between two individuals' (Collins, 1993: 123).

In recent decades mentoring has been associated with career development and professional socialisation in a variety of occupational settings. Many studies have looked at the development of formal and informal mentoring for managers and executives in business, industry and public sector organisations (e.g. Collins and Scott, 1978; Clawson, 1980 and Kram, 1985). Mentorship has also increasingly come to be seen as an aspect of staff development and training in social work (Taibbi, 1983), nursing (Hernandez-Piloto Brito, 1992) and teaching (McIntyre et al., 1993).

Mentoring is not only concerned with the building of supportive relationships between supervisors and trainees to ensure that the latter develop the requisite knowledge and skills to become competent practitioners in their own right. In fact it has become popular across a range of disciplines and in a variety of social and institutional contexts. On a fundamental level, a mentor can be viewed as playing a significant role in a young person's transition from adolescence to adulthood (Levinson et al., 1978; Hamilton 1991; Gottlieb and Sylvestre, 1994). It is in this more general context of adult maturation and the development of essential interpersonal skills and behavioural competencies that mentoring has come to be seen as a way of helping vulnerable young people. The theoretical foundation for such a view is found within developmental psychology (Hamilton and Darling, 1989).

The marked rise in the popularity of mentoring in the USA in the closing decades of the last century has been well documented (Freedman, 1993). In the case of disadvantaged youth, policy-makers and programme providers see mentoring as an effective way of compensating vulnerable young people for a variety of perceived inadequacies in areas such as family life, parental support and educational provision (Rhodes et al., 1992). A similar view has emerged in the UK. Here, in recent years, mentoring has become an increasingly popular form of social intervention, especially when dealing with disaffected and disadvantaged young people. Mentoring schemes feature as an important element in a number of policies and programmes designed with the intention of tackling the wider problem of social exclusion. In particular, mentoring has gained wide-spread support in the fields of education and training and youth justice.

As far as youth crime is concerned, it has been suggested that adult mentors can offer young people from unstable family environments an alternative source of practical help, emotional support, guidance and care, as well as provide them with a positive role model (Home Office, 1997). In this sense mentoring can form part of a wider preventative strategy, which, in the long run, is recognised as constituting an efficient and effective means of tackling youth crime (Audit Commission, 1996). The significance attached to mentoring as part of this general strategy is indicated by the fact that the Youth Justice Board is currently supporting around 40 innovative mentoring projects throughout the country.

Research findings from the USA suggest that mentoring can have a positive impact on the lives of young people. For example, an impact study of the Big Brothers/Big Sisters programme, which compared a group of young people who had received mentoring with a matched control group, concluded that those who had had the benefit of a mentor were 46 per cent less likely to take illegal drugs and 37 per cent less likely to skip school (Tierney et al., 1995). An evaluative study of Partners for Youth, an intergenerational mentoring project for high-risk middle school students in Philadelphia, found that participants showed signs of improvement in a number of areas such as their relationships with adults and peers, their general classroom behaviour and their attitudes towards substance misuse (source: National Mentoring Partnership). While there have been fewer studies of mentoring schemes in the UK, what little research has been undertaken has yielded positive results. For example, Porteous (1998) in an evaluation of the Community Service Volunteers On-Line Mentoring Scheme reported a number of positive outcomes: these included a reduction in offending behaviour, a reduction in problems experienced at school and an improvement in the self-confidence and self-esteem of mentees. In a more recent study of primary school children preliminary findings revealed that both parents and teachers observed positive changes in the children's behaviour, claiming that they were better behaved, more controlled, more confident and better able to communicate their feelings and emotions. There was also some evidence of an improvement in academic work (Roberts and Singh, 1999).

By and large, the structure and organisation of mentoring support roles can vary markedly from one mentoring scheme to another. Indeed, as Philip and Hendry (1996) illustrated in their study of how young people perceived the mentoring relationship, mentoring can take a number of different forms. In any one project, the nature, structure and content of the mentoring role is determined by a number of factors, such as the specific aims and objectives of the programme, the perceived needs and problems experienced by the target group of potential mentees, the nature of the institutional or community context in which the scheme operates and the resources available for supporting mentoring work.

Mentoring forms one of the key components of the Dalston project. Indeed, the development of a successful mentoring relationship is an integral feature of the overall programme. Basically, the idea is that volunteer mentors develop structured, one-to-one relationships that focus on the individual needs of the young person concerned.

Recruitment and selection

The project started recruiting volunteer mentors for Year 1 towards the end of 1996 and in this respect had the advantage of being able to draw upon the experience of the first Dalston Youth Project, aimed at 15-to 18 year-olds, which was launched in 1994. In fact recruitment for both projects was carried out simultaneously. Advertisements for volunteers were placed in a wide range of publications including *The Guardian*, *The Hackney Gazette*, *The Voice*, *The Big Issue*, *Ms London* and a Turkish newspaper. In addition, notices were placed in local libraries, shops, banks and building societies in order to attract potential volunteers from the local community. Anyone responding to the advertisements and expressing interest in becoming a mentor was invited to an open evening to meet informally with project staff and hear about the scheme and its principal aims and objectives.

Research has shown that a critical factor in the creation of successful mentoring relationships is undoubtedly the actions and attitudes of the mentors themselves (Morrow and Styles, 1995). Therefore, careful screening of applicants is essential. All volunteers were subjected to a screening process, the primary purpose of which was to protect young people by identifying and screening out any unsuitable applicants. The selection process began with the applicant completing a standard Volunteer Mentor's Application Form. This requested basic information regarding the applicant's socio-demographic characteristics and other relevant background details. For example, applicants were asked about their previous involvement in voluntary work and if they had any specific skills particularly relevant to working with young people. Applicants were also required to disclose information about all criminal convictions, both current and spent, and were informed that they would be subjected to a police check. Applicants were not automatically ruled out if they had a previous conviction for a criminal offence, as factors such as the nature of the offence and when it took place were taken into account. The purpose of the exercise was to protect young people by screening out any volunteers who posed a safety risk.

The application form also contained questions about the applicant's general availability, their perception of the needs of young people in the local community, their reasons for wanting to be a mentor and how they would help children at risk and deal with difficult situations.

Following the completion of an application form and an interview with a member of the project team, successful applicants were invited to take part in the initial training for mentors. As described below, this training took place over two weekends, during the course of which volunteers were observed to see if they displayed the kind of attitudes and interpersonal skills essential for forming and developing positive relationships with young people. Project staff also used the residential weekend, when prospective mentors and mentees took part in a variety of group activities, to observe how well individual volunteers interacted with young people. While the residential weekend played an important part in the matching process, as described below, more fundamentally it also helped in the selection process by identifying any volunteers who might not be ideally suited for mentoring a young person who displayed challenging behaviour.

The recruitment and selection procedures adopted brought forward sufficient mentors for the project in the first three years. In total 80 mentors were recruited and completed initial training during this period. However, because of the rapidly increasing number of mentoring projects throughout the country, recruiting enough suitable mentors has recently become much more difficult. At the end of the three-year period, when recruitment was underway for Year 4, DYP II encountered difficulties in recruiting a sufficient number of mentors.

Profile of mentors

Of the 80 mentors recruited, background information was available on 71. Information was not available on seven mentors in Year 1 who were not prominent after the residential weekend (because they or their mentee withdrew from the project) nor on two mentors in Year 3 who had been mentors on the older DYP I project and did not need to complete the application form. As Table 4 shows, 51 (of the 71) mentors were female and 20 were male. The lack of male mentors was viewed as disappointing and the project did make attempts to recruit more male mentors but to no avail. Attracting sufficient numbers of male volunteers is a problem faced by many mentoring schemes. The age distribution of mentors revealed that the majority fell within the 20 – 30 year age range. The self-defined ethnic status of mentors is presented in Table 5. The majority of mentors were from ethnic minority backgrounds, a distribution that reflected the ethnic composition of the mentees.

Table 4: Age and sex of mentors

Year		20-24	25-29	30-34	35-39	40-45	All ages
Year 1	Male	-	2	2	2	2	8
	Female	6	2	4	-	-	12
Year 2	Male	1	1	2	-	1	5
	Female	3	7	5	5	-	20*
Year 3	Male	-	1	3	2	1	7
	Female	-	11	4	3	-	18
Total		10	24	20	12	4	70

*One female mentor did not disclose her age.

Table 5: Ethnic background of mentors*

Year	Asian	African	Afro-Caribbean	Black	Caribbean	West Indian	White	Other	Total
Year 1	-	2	3	6	2	-	5	2	20
Year 2	1	3	2	9	1	3	7	-	26
Year 3	2	5	4	-	2	2	8	2	25
Total	3	10	9	15	5	5	20	4	71

* The ethnic categories used in this table are based on the responses of mentors to an open-ended question on ethnicity.

Mentors were drawn from a wide range of socio-cultural backgrounds, reflecting the socio-demographic profile and multi-ethnic composition of the local community. As regards their occupational backgrounds, just over three-quarters of volunteers were in full-time employment. The majority of these fell into two broad occupational categories: 22 were employed in general administrative and clerical jobs and 16 worked in the human services sector, particularly in the areas of social welfare and teaching. Of the remainder, six mentors were in professional/managerial posts in public sector organisations (e.g. accountancy, retail management), a further six were skilled manual workers (e.g. chef, engineer) and three were engaged in unskilled manual work. Eighteen mentors were not engaged in full-time employment, of these seven worked part-time, five were students and six were unemployed when they began mentoring.

The vast majority of mentors reported having undertaken some form of voluntary work in the past. In Year 1, 85 per cent of mentors reported a history of volunteering, the comparable figures for Year 2 and Year 3 were 76 per cent and 80 per cent respectively. Many mentors had experience of more than one type of voluntary work. Of the 20 mentors in Year 3, 17 had previous experience of voluntary work with young people and of these, five had been involved in mentoring or befriending schemes.

Mentors' motivations

Mentors across all three cohorts gave a variety of reasons for applying to join DYP II. Although there was some variation in the mixture of reasons given at the individual level, a number of broad themes emerged. By and large, the motivations for wanting to take up mentoring were primarily focused around wanting to help disadvantaged young people. As the following comments illustrate, some mentors gave altruistic reasons for joining the project:

> "My education was very frustrating, I had problems at home and so forth. So I want to share my experiences with problem kids of today and help them."

> "I want to be a mentor because I've been through a lot of what these young people are going through and have experience (to offer)."

> "I would like to do something positive with my free time, helping others and giving back to society."

In some cases it was not only a wish to do something 'useful', but a desire to try and help someone overcome the kinds of problems and difficulties the mentors themselves had experienced in their own teenage years.

As well as providing an opportunity for them to help someone else, many mentors also saw mentoring as important in terms of their own personal development. This was illustrated in the following:

> "I believe it (mentoring) would help me to look within myself and challenge my own views and attitudes to young people."

> "Being a mentor helps you focus and reflect on your own behaviour and actions. It puts a different perspective on your problems."

For some, mentoring was also seen as a way of making a worthwhile contribution while at the same time gaining knowledge and experience that would be of benefit to them in terms of their future careers.

> "I hope to broaden my counselling experience and to improve my chances of going into a career in youth and community work."

"I think I can benefit by getting experience with young people. I want to be a mentor as I hope to qualify as a social worker and think I most probably want to work with young people possibly, in youth justice."

"I am interested in becoming a career counsellor and will be starting a part-time course in April. Being a mentor will equip me with experience of dealing and meeting the needs of young people, thus helping them in choosing the right career."

Induction, training and support

In each of the three years of the project the initial training and induction of the mentors took place over two weekends, in January and February, prior to the residential weekend. The first weekend of training for each cohort of mentors was organised by Vernon Simpson Associates and the programme covered the following topic areas:

- What is mentoring?

- Qualities of successful mentors

- Young people and their needs

- Young people in families

- Oppression

- Values, differences and conflict

- Interpersonal communication

- Abuse

- Bullying

The sessions were designed not only to convey information but also to encourage active learning and group participation in a workshop setting. The sessions were lively and much appreciated by the participants.

The second weekend of training was organised and run by project staff. The primary aim was to provide an orientation for volunteers in which the rules, requirements and philosophy of DYP II was explained. The project tutors outlined the educational classes and how mentors could help mentees with their educational development. The day was very interactive, with mentors raising many questions regarding their role and responsibilities. There was much discussion around such topics as the kinds of activities they could undertake with their mentees and how to draw boundaries around issues, events and behaviours.

The initial training programme provided a broad introduction to the fundamental aspects of mentoring and gave participants a general feel for some of the main issues surrounding working with young people. From observation and interviews with mentors there was evidence that the initial training course was well received. In addition, towards the end of the twelve-month mentoring period the project sent each mentor a Mentoring Programme Evaluation Questionnaire to complete. The general purpose of this questionnaire was to obtain feedback from mentors on their general experiences of mentoring and their perceptions of the training and support they had received from the project over the previous twelve months. Although only a small number of mentors returned completed questionnaires, the responses were positive.

All the mentors who either were interviewed or returned questionnaires said that they had found the initial training course extremely useful. The majority of volunteers had no previous experience of mentoring and many commented that the initial training gave them a good insight into what to expect from a mentoring relationship. Responses such as the following were fairly typical from mentors:

"The training course was extensive, really useful, it gives you a good insight into how young people think and view the world. Without it I would have been at a bit of a loss."

"For me it (the training) *gave me a good idea of what to expect...the kind of problems I might come across and how best I might help...it made you aware of the fact that mentoring is challenging."*

"(The training course) clarified very well the role of a mentor and the limits and boundaries of that role."

Across all three years of the project there was a general consensus among mentors that the initial training had provided adequate and sufficient preparation for the task of mentoring.

During the first year of the project the evaluators noted, from interviews and informal discussions with mentors, that although there was a general appreciation of the initial training programme there was an expressed need for further support and continued training throughout the mentoring period. One referred to *"a sense of drifting away from the project"* and thought that *"mentors had not been embraced by the project"*. Continued support would have been welcomed by many, and, they suggested, it would have been a way of keeping others 'on board'. To arrest the decline in interest one thought that there ought to have been more organised group events such as repeats of the residential weekend rather than *"meetings around a formica table"*, which was his way of describing mentor evenings at the Round Chapel (the DYP II centre).

The project responded by creating a new part-time post for a mentor support worker. Unfortunately the first person appointed did not take up the position and it was not until the end of the first year that the post was successfully filled.

As previous research has shown, one of the main challenges facing mentoring schemes is the need to develop and strengthen their infrastructures so as to enable them to provide the practical support and administrative back-up necessary for mentoring relationships to flourish (Tierney and Branch, 1992; Tierney et al., 1995). In the case of DYP II the role of mentor co-ordinator became an integral feature of the programme's infrastructure. One of the tasks undertaken by the mentor co-ordinator was to arrange a programme of regular training sessions for mentors. Some of these sessions addressed practical issues specific to mentoring, such as how to encourage young people to set themselves personal goals, how to help raise their self-esteem and how to bring a mentoring relationship to a satisfactory conclusion. Other sessions focused on substantive topics among which were included substance misuse, domestic violence and young people and sexual identity.

By the third year of the evaluation period training sessions were being held on a monthly basis and were incorporated in the mentor support evenings. Where appropriate, guest speakers were invited to address specialist topics. Attendance at individual mentor training and support sessions varied from between five and 12 mentors. Those who did attend reported that they found the sessions extremely helpful and informative, as the following comments illustrate:

"Discussing problems and worries with other mentors was very reassuring and served to re-motivate me. I found workshops on careers, sexual health and drugs useful because contacts for further information and help were offered."

"The monthly training sessions were useful for two reasons: it was a forum for mentors to meet and draw support and the topics covered complemented the Goldsmiths College course contents."

The Goldsmiths College course referred to above leads to a Certificate of Professional Practice in Mentoring and is an accredited course organised by Vernon Simpson Associates. The course is held at Goldsmiths College, University of London. Part way through Year 2 eight mentors enrolled on this course; in Year 3 twelve mentors took part in the course.

In addition to the formal training sessions and mentor support evenings, mentors were also able to discuss informally with project staff any problems or concerns they had regarding their mentees. The accessibility and helpfulness of members of the project team were very much appreciated by the mentors interviewed. In cases where mentors had to deal with young people who were facing extremely difficult family circumstances, necessary extra support was provided on a one-to-one basis. Having a mentor co-ordinator in place not only meant that there was routine monitoring of mentor-mentee contacts, but also ensured that where mentors encountered difficulties there was someone on hand to make sure that the necessary support was forthcoming.

Clearly, the establishment of the part-time post of mentor co-ordinator was a key development and did much to overcome the concerns expressed by mentors in Year 1 who felt remote and isolated from the project and in need of additional support. The mentor co-ordinator did much not only to support mentors but also to encourage them to attend the monthly training sessions and other activities organised by the project.

Matching mentor to mentee

The responsibility for matching mentors to mentees rested with the project co-ordinator, although all members of the project team (in particular the mentor co-ordinator when in post) played a part in the process. Profiles of prospective mentors, highlighting their personal qualities, background and interests, were obtained from the Volunteer Mentor's Application Form and information gleaned from selection interviews. The two weekend training courses also provided an opportunity for staff to undertake informal assessments of volunteers. Referral forms from the schools and a short questionnaire completed by the young people, eliciting information on their interests and expectations from a mentor, provided the project co-ordinator with information about each young person joining the project. In consultation with other project staff, the project co-ordinator then notionally matched mentors and mentees, but at this stage did not inform either party. The residential weekend was used to introduce mentors to young people generally. The groups undertaking the activities were constructed so as to bring each potential mentor-mentee pairing together. If a good relationship did not appear to be developing then there was time during the weekend to test out alternative pairings. In Years 1 and 2 the project team discussed the final matches on Saturday evening and on the Sunday afternoon mentors and mentees were told who had been assigned to whom. The final session thus enabled mentors and mentees to get together to identify common interests and arrange subsequent meetings. Because of the problems experienced in Year 2 when not all mentees attended the residential weekend, in Year 3 the announcement of pairings took place at a 'Games Evening' one week after the residential.

The mentoring relationship

In order to gain an insight into the mentoring process information on how mentoring relationships were created and developed was obtained from five main sources:

- attending mentor support evenings and listening to mentors discuss their mentoring experiences;

- conversations with mentors during casual encounters at events and activities organised by the project;

- face-to-face or telephone interviews with individual mentors;

- interviews with young people; and

- interviews with relevant project staff.

From fieldwork observations and interviews early on in the first year it was discovered that a number of mentors were experiencing difficulties at the outset in establishing a relationship and in identifying the scope of the mentoring role. One mentioned the initial difficulty of meeting the mentee's family. The parents were suspicious and were only forthcoming when they were reassured that the mentor was not from an official agency such as the police or social services. This mentor felt that the project could have done more to 'pave the way'.

Other mentors were uncertain as to exactly where the boundaries lay. One mentor related an experience where she had taken the young person ice skating. The mentor had agreed with the parents when they would be returning home but the young person met friends at the ice rink and did not want to leave at the appointed time. The mentor felt a conflict of loyalties between the mentee and his parents. To get 'heavy' could have jeopardised her relationship with the mentee, but to be late returning would have caused distress to the parents. Another mentor said that she felt her mentee lacked 'family life' and was tempted to take him to her *"gran's who would be welcoming and where there would be lots of people"*. However, she wondered whether this would be overstepping the mark by effectively 'fostering' the mentee and undermining his relationship with his own family.

A particular issue arose over the mentors' relations with the schools. Many mentors felt that they could make a contribution to their mentee's education and indeed felt that to be part of their role. They therefore wanted to contact the school to find out how their efforts might best be directed. This issue would have benefited from prior thought by the project and it should have been anticipated that the schools might see this as being intrusive. Mentors were subsequently advised not to focus on educational matters but to address questions pertaining to 'overall lifestyle'. Many had adopted this role anyway. As one mentor noted:

"I'm not there to provide a role model but more guidance, as a friend. It's important to 'keep it tight', be just a friend and avoid getting in too deep."

Another said:

"[I'm] not there to rattle his cage but be there for him."

With the introduction of mentor support evenings and the eventual development of regular training sessions throughout the mentoring period, these initial concerns about the boundaries of the mentoring role were addressed.

The mentoring model encouraged by the project was oriented towards developing the young person and not just addressing the current problems they faced. While mentors saw themselves as befriending a young person in difficult circumstances, thus providing mentees with an opportunity to discuss their problems with someone who did not constitute an authority figure, they also considered themselves to have a significant part to play in helping young people to improve their self-esteem. To this end, mentors were encouraged to find out what their mentees were interested in and then help them to find ways of pursuing that interest. Many mentors arranged with their mentees to visit museums, art galleries, cinemas and sports centres. This was both a way of facilitating mentees' access to a range of leisure, social and cultural pursuits and a means of providing an informal setting in which a mentoring relationship could be cultivated.

The mentors interviewed during the course of the evaluation tended to be the more active and enthusiastic ones. They were the ones who attended mentor support evenings, frequently visited the project centre, took part in activities organised by the project and contributed to the Newsletter. It was from these mentors that it was possible to get an idea of how the nature of the mentoring role and its potential benefits were perceived. In this respect, four key observations are worthy of note, as they have implications for what might be considered to constitute 'good practice' as far as establishing a successful mentoring relationship is concerned.

Firstly, mentors stressed the importance of not being overtly judgmental at the outset of a relationship, but of listening to the young person and gradually winning his or her trust and confidence. As one mentor (Year 3) commented, "*Be yourself. Don't try to be a specific role model. Just relax and don't try to be someone you are not*". While it was recognised that different approaches were needed with different young people, it was commonly acknowledged that in all cases it was important to be patient and not to try to project a particular ideal image of oneself.

Secondly, while mentors recognised the importance of finding something that their mentees were good at and then giving them praise and encouragement, they also saw it as part of their responsibility to question and challenge inappropriate behaviour. This was done largely by helping the young person to see their actions and conduct from the perspective of significant others. Mentors also talked about helping their mentees to explore alternative ways of dealing with problems and difficulties. In such circumstances, striking the right balance between teaching and befriending was seen to be important. For example, as one mentor noted,

> "If I think he's done wrong, yeh, then I tell him, but I do it as one friend to another, I don't get all heavy...I tell him why I think he's in the wrong...and then we discuss how he could have handled things better".

In this case the mentee had a reputation for getting into fights at school, claiming that he was provoked by the name-calling he received from certain pupils. The mentor described how he explained that violence was not an appropriate reaction and discussed with his mentee ways in which he could control his temper or avoid certain situations in future.

Thirdly, mentors were conscious of the need to encourage their mentees to take decisions and set themselves achievable goals. When deciding what to do and where to go when they met, many mentors involved their mentees in the decision-making. Visits or activities could be for general recreation, such as going to the cinema, or they could have a more specific purpose. A good example of the latter was provided by one mentor who discovered that his mentee had an interest in jazz music. Consequently, he arranged a visit to see a music tutor at Goldsmiths College who talked to the mentee about opportunities for studying music after leaving school and emphasised the importance of working hard in order to reach a good standard in preparation for further study.

In terms of setting goals, some mentors encouraged their mentees to set themselves personal targets. These differed from one individual to another, examples being handing in homework on time, regular attendance at the educational classes and not getting involved in fights at school.

Finally, a common theme that emerged from the data was the idea that the mentoring relationship was very much a reciprocal relationship. Frequently mentors referred to the benefits they enjoyed as a result of mentoring. The following is a typical example:

> "It (mentoring) has helped me to relax, to slow down my pace of life... I have never worked with someone my mentee's age before, I share things with him I didn't share with my own son and it's helped me to mellow out".

This notion of mentoring as a highly reciprocal set of processes which benefit both parties has been observed elsewhere (Philip and Hendry, 2000).

As previously noted, research shows that the actions and attitudes of mentors are critical factors in establishing successful mentoring relationships (Morrow and Styles, 1995). Communicating with young people, gaining their trust and establishing a mutually satisfying relationship calls for specific personal qualities on the part of the mentor. The mentors interviewed recognised the importance of empathy between the mentor and mentee and the need to exercise patience in developing the mentoring relationship. The mentoring co-ordinator neatly identified the qualities a mentor needs as "kindness, patience and persistence".

Mentee's perceptions of mentoring

Commenting upon mentoring research Philip and Hendry note that 'there have been few accounts given by young people themselves about their experiences, expectations and understandings of (mentoring) processes' (1996: 190). In the current study semi-structured interviews with young people were undertaken in order to address this issue and obtain an insight into how mentoring is seen to work from the young person's perspective.

When asked what a mentor was, none of the young people who were interviewed had any difficulty in describing the role and functions of a mentor. The following are a few examples:

> "A mentor is your own personal person. You can talk to that person and they won't tell anybody else. They are like a second sister or brother. A really, really good friend. They help you with your education."

> "A person that can teach you ... a bit like another parent."

> "Your own tutor ... teaches you what she thinks you need."

> "A mentor is someone who is like a friend ... someone who helps you."

> "You can use a mentor in different ways. The way I use my mentor... [is to] talk things through. I have no one to talk to at home."

What immediately emerges from these descriptions is the notion that the role of an adult mentor is seen as being multi-faceted and possessing some of the characteristics associated with the more formalised roles of parent and teacher. However, while a mentor is seen as a potential source of advice and guidance, she or he is not viewed as an authority figure but is seen as a friend.

Many of the young people interviewed were particularly appreciative of the perceived willingness of their mentors to listen to them talk about their problems without being overly judgmental. They felt that they could talk to them in a way that they could not talk to their parents or schoolteachers. However, this did not imply that mentees saw their mentors as nothing more than sympathetic listeners. As one interviewee remarked:

> "He [mentor] will tell me when he thinks I'm in the wrong ... but at least he listens to what I've got to say."

For these individuals the mentoring relationship was a successful and rewarding experience. As one interviewee remarked:

"The best thing about this project is my mentor ... I've got the best mentor. He's met my parents and they think he's great."

Extent of engagement

How many mentoring relationships lasted the full twelve months and how often mentors and mentees met was difficult to establish with any precision, particularly during Year 1. The project initially asked mentors to keep diaries in which to record the number of meetings they had with their mentees and the kinds of activities they undertook together. However, this system of record keeping did not prove successful, as mentors did not see any form of record keeping as a priority. This was not an uncommon finding and applies in other areas of voluntary work. Volunteers give their free time to do what interests or motivates them; they do not give priority to an organisation's need to formally measure and assess performance. Assessment of the success of mentoring or the degree of participation is thus impressionistic, based on interviews with mentors, mentees and project staff.

From interviews with a cross-section of mentors and young people in Year 1 it appeared that about one-half of the mentees met their mentor regularly throughout the one-year period. They said that they met once a week and sometimes more often. However, there was evidence that the frequency of contacts declined during the year. Initially contacts were once a week, as prescribed by the project, but over time they became less frequent, with once a month becoming more typical.

One-half of relationships did not succeed. There were various reasons for this. Some young people did not wish to proceed (for example, five young people in the first year did not engage with the project after the residential weekend). Some mentors left the project because they moved away from the area or had other commitments, and some mentors and mentees, despite careful matching at the outset, found that they did not 'get on'. Where there was difficulty establishing a suitable relationship another mentor was assigned to the mentee. For example, one young person interviewed had not been able to establish a successful relationship with the first mentor assigned to her. The second mentor she was given never managed to meet her and was also replaced.

While it was not possible to say exactly how many mentoring relationships were successful in Year 1, 15 mentors were awarded certificates of commendation at Graduation Night (discussed later), which suggested that approximately 50 per cent of the relationships maintained some level of contact throughout the year. This figure would accord with information gleaned from the interviews and the observations of the evaluators. A basic core of about a dozen mentors would turn up to mentor evenings and one or two more were absent only because of work commitments.

The project's monitoring of mentoring relationships improved in Years 2 and 3 with the appointment of the mentoring co-ordinator. The co-ordinator kept in close contact with mentors by means of monthly telephone calls and regular meetings. Mentoring statistics for Years 2 and 3 are presented in Table 6.

Table 6: Mentoring statistics for Years 2 and 3

	Year 2	Year 3
Completed initial training	27	25
Attended residential weekend	27	22
Released immediately after residential weekend	1	0
Left immediately after residential weekend	1	0
Joined after residential weekend	1	2
Started mentoring	26	27
Did not complete mentoring (left after starting)	7	11
Released from mentoring (mentee withdrew)	3	2
Awarded mentoring certificate	16	14

As these figures show, not all the mentor volunteers stayed with the project for the full twelve-month period. In Year 2 two mentors left immediately after the residential weekend, one was released because he was considered unsuitable and another was difficult to contact and was presumed to have left. Of those who did not complete a twelve-month cycle of mentoring, some resigned for personal reasons. For example, in Year 3 five mentors resigned; two due to the pressure of other commitments, two because they moved from the area and one as a result of poor health. A further six volunteers did not actually resign but failed to make the necessary commitment and were therefore not considered eligible for a mentoring certificate. In Year 2 three mentors, and in Year 3 two mentors, had to be released because their mentees failed to engage with the project.

At the end of Year 3 a total of 14 mentors were awarded a certificate in recognition of their contribution to the mentoring component; 16 mentors had been awarded the certificate the previous year. However, one or two mentors received a certificate for their commitment to mentoring and to the project even though the relationship with their mentee had broken down because the mentee withdrew. Nevertheless, in terms of project outputs about a half of the mentor-mentee matches were successful.

5   Educational Component

As a primary aim of the project was to re-motivate those on the verge of dropping out of mainstream schooling and to improve their basic numeracy and literacy skills, the educational component was seen as a key aspect of the project. Over the course of the three years the educational component evolved and adapted as a result of the experience gained by the project, the changing needs of the young people and in response to staff turnover and other logistical and practical issues. It is not the purpose of this report to document all the minute details but to present the major developments and lessons learned.

The plan of the project was to provide each young person with six hours' tuition after school each week during term time. Initially this was delivered as three two-hour sessions but later became two three-hour sessions. Each of the three cohorts was split into three groups so that in Years 1 and 2 the girls (from Girls School) formed one class, the Year 9 boys (from Boys School) another and the Year 8 boys (from Boys School) the third. In Year 3 the three classes comprised the girls, the Year 8 boys from Boys School and the Year 8 boys from Mixed School. Three part-time tutors were initially recruited (initially working 12 hours per week), with one tutor being assigned to each class.

An issue that needed to be addressed at the outset was the location of the after-school classes. The original project plan was to locate the educational component on school premises. This would facilitate closer contact with the school and enable the project to work with the school in achieving its aims of re-integrating the young people back into mainstream schooling.

Girls School agreed to have the after-school classes take place 'on-site', although it was never entirely comfortable with this arrangement. The school mentioned logistical problems; all other after-school activities lasted for one hour and special arrangements had to be made to accommodate the longer DYP sessions. There was also the legal issue, never resolved, of who – the school or DYP – was responsible for the girls' safety and well-being. Primarily because of demands on space within the school, Boys School did not host the after-school sessions. Thus at the beginning of Year 1, the after-school classes for the girls were held at the girls' school and the educational programme for the boys took place at the DYP centre. One tutor was thus based at Girls School and two tutors were based at the DYP premises.

Although the initial intention was to locate the after-school classes on school premises a view emerged early on (and by the end of the three years had become a firm consensus) that to be successful the educational component needed to be held away from the school. This, it was felt, would ensure that DYP had a separate identity and was not seen simply as extra schooling. A separate identity would be more appropriate in addressing student perceptions, disaffection and alienation from the day school. In addition, the young people would have a greater sense of belonging to the project and of having ownership of it. They would also feel less inhibited in setting the project's agenda and defining its activities. As one school representative said, simply being on first-name terms with the tutors at DYP, which was easier to instigate off-site, could make a significant difference to the young people's attitudes. In mainstream school formal terms of address had to be adhered to.

The difficulties experienced by Girls School, coupled with the falling attendance of the girls in the early part of the first year, provided some support for the view that the educational component should be located off-site. There was also some evidence to suggest that the girls themselves were envious of the boys having their classes at DYP. Matters came to a head in the summer term of the first year when the tutor at Girls School resigned and it was less easy for the project to deploy tutors across three classes when one class was held at a different location. In the final term of the first year of the project the girls class was relocated to the DYP premises and in Years 2 and 3 all three classes were held at DYP premises.

Resources and staffing

By the end of the first year, and throughout the two subsequent years, DYP had access to one dedicated classroom and one other room which could be used as a classroom. Over the period the project developed its learning resources. The project was well provided with computers and software, stationery and equipment, but tutors felt that there was a lack of reading books of different levels that would be of interest to the young people attending the classes. Each young person in the Year 3 cohort was given a large diary and encouraged to write in it anything that he or she felt to be important. Time was set aside each lesson and the diary became a significant feature of the project. The young people sometimes wrote moving and harrowing accounts of their lives and the diary became an effective means of communication with project staff.

The turnover of tutors proved to be a particular issue. Over the three-year period, nine tutors were engaged by the project. Only three tutors stayed for more than one year. Not all tutors resigned from the project when they ceased to be tutors. Two were transferred to other posts within DYP – one tutor became DYP director and the other took up the post of project co-ordinator when that became vacant. Both provided essential continuity and cover during particularly difficult periods.

There were perhaps several contributory factors to the high turnover of staff. First, it is difficult to recruit and retain teachers in disadvantaged inner-city areas. Schools in this kind of area face extreme problems and DYP's experience simply mirrored the more general problem. However, the part-time nature of the posts, coupled with the hours the tutors had to work, exacerbated the situation. Part-time employment made the job attractive only to those who already had other part-time work or to those who were looking for temporary employment until they found full-time work. For example, several tutors left to take up full-time employment elsewhere. Working after school hours also made the posts unattractive to a large pool of potential applicants such as teachers with young families returning from a career break, seeking work during that part of the day when their own children were at school. In the latter part of the project, staff morale was affected by adverse relations with their employer, Crime Concern. There were delays and difficulties over remunerating staff for the hours they had worked and this certainly undermined two tutors' long term commitment to their posts.

At the end of the three-year period, when one of the two remaining part-time tutors resigned (to take up a full-time post in a school) the project appointed a full-time tutor.

Of the nine tutors engaged during the three years, four were women and five were men. Five were from ethnic minority backgrounds. Between them they had a range of experience in youth work, education and training. Only one had limited experience of working with young people.

The high turnover of staff, resulting in periods when posts were vacant, inevitably caused disruption to the planning and delivery of the education component (not to mention the considerable time, effort and money that had to be devoted to recruiting new staff). The initial plan of assigning one tutor to each group often had to be abandoned, and classes were sometimes merged as more flexible arrangements were needed. Some administrative procedures were delayed, such as the introduction of attendance records, the formal testing and re-testing of participants and the drawing up of detailed Individual Education Plans (IEPs) for each young person. Liaison with schools was adversely affected and the planning and content of classes had to be revised frequently.

There was, however, a positive outcome. Tutors began to work more collaboratively. This collective approach was facilitated by the second project co-ordinator who had been a tutor at DYP and before that a school head. He initiated more formal procedures to plan the content of the educational component. Tutors were no longer assigned to classes but rotated between them. Not only did this minimise discontinuity to a class when its tutor left but it also provided the young people with variety. It also reduced the possibility – which occurred on one occasion – of a class disintegrating when the relationship between the tutor and the young people broke down.

At this point more formal procedures were developed and introduced; for example, registers of attendance were kept. The young people and project staff entered into an informal contract at the start of the project, which underpinned commitments on either side. Young people agreed to participate in a positive way and to be respectful to others. Tutors would, in turn, treat the young people with respect and help them learn and to achieve the targets set in their IEPs which were drawn up at the outset of the project. The plan listed the student's interests and identified his or her academic strengths and areas to be developed. Realistic targets were set, such as learning a particular 'times table' or learning to spell a certain number of words per week. Behaviour and social skills were also addressed. The IEP was formally reviewed half way through the year where the young person was given feedback and a report was written on each young person.

The after-school classes

At the outset it was recognised that in order to engage disaffected young people the education component had to be different from mainstream schooling. If it was too formal it would be seen as no different from mainstream school and the young people would stay away. On the other hand, DYP was not to be a Youth Club. An emphasis was placed on educational objectives. A balance had to be struck. In addition, the education component placed an emphasis on rewarding achievement and building up self-esteem.

The tutors were asked what particular problems the young people posed and why they thought those on the project had not been succeeding in mainstream school. The tutors felt that the problems were more of a personal rather than an educational nature. Starting with disadvantages, the young people had fallen behind at school. An inevitable cycle of decline then took hold. They became aggressive and disruptive to cover up their failings. They then formed peer groups which reinforced that it was not 'cool' to conform or succeed at school. The schools' reaction was to minimise the degree of disruption these students caused to other pupils and to the school generally. The initial priorities for the tutors at DYP, they said, were to stimulate an interest in education and learning and to confront the aggressive behaviour in order that the young people could begin to function as a class. The young people had to 'learn how to learn'.

Outwardly and collectively the young people were dismissive of education. They felt that their school had a negative view of them: "they [schools] only tell us when we are doing wrong". However, privately and individually the young people confessed to not being able to read, write or 'do maths'. This embarrassed them and as a consequence they had low self-esteem. At the beginning, in class all the young people were reluctant to undertake tasks which would reveal their limitations. It was important, therefore, to develop a culture in which no one was 'laughed at' for making mistakes.

Tutors played to their own strengths and drew on their professional knowledge and experience in approaching the behavioural and educational challenges presented by the young people. Two tutors were qualified practitioners of neuro-linguistic programming (NLP) and both incorporated this approach into their teaching. NLP attempts to identify and define how a person's mind works, and this knowledge can be used to help that person develop more effective ways of learning. The NLP approach was carefully planned and delivered and was used, for example, to encourage individual methods of remembering spellings. Flash cards were used and the young people were encouraged to use pictorial and colour association to help with their learning. Questions like, "Where do you see the word?", "Can you see it in your head?", "Is it in the window?" were constantly asked. They were also asked to spell words forwards and backwards.

Although some of the methods used may seem unconventional to mainstream teachers, the young people responded well, and some appeared to be achieving in an area which they had previously found difficult. Similar methods were also used for those struggling with numeracy. 'Tables games' were played, often in pairs.

Discussions around anger took place in which the young people talked about what made them angry. They were asked how they could recognise their anger. For example, "Do you see a colour?", "Do you feel any thing inside?" All the responses the young people made in these areas were discussed and they were encouraged to use them at school to help them with their work and control anger, etc.

One of the tutors gave information to teachers at the schools about NLP and its potential in helping young people experiencing difficulties with education.

Examples of classes

Three examples of after-school classes are given in order to provide a flavour of the kinds of subjects covered and the way the classes were structured. The tutors placed emphasis on involving the young people in the design and content of classes.

Class 1

The centrepiece of the class was a video about a black American basketball player who had started life in a poor neighbourhood, had not engaged with school and began drifting into crime. His ability at basketball eventually brought him success but only after considerable commitment and dedication and a good deal of hard work.

The tutor stopped the video at key moments to discuss how the basketball player had coped with setbacks and achievements, how he had dealt with competition between friends and how success had changed his life.

Before and after the video, the boys wrote in their diaries and prepared posters for the forthcoming presentation evening. One also prepared a contribution for the next Newsletter. Much of the material was prepared on computer.

Class 2

The girls' classes also included writing in diaries, preparing posters for presentation evenings and contributions for the Newsletter. However, many of the girls were interested in dance and drama and they spent some time devising and rehearsing plays and preparing and practising dance routines. With the boys they jointly prepared food for special events.

In one class the tutor read extracts from a book by a successful black female writer. At appropriate points in the lesson the girls would discuss the issues raised in the book. On another occasion the tutor handed out a sheet containing the words of a song. The words of the song had been altered – some had been mis-spelt and grammatical errors had been introduced. The girls' task was to correct all the mistakes.

Class 3

In one class, attended by five Year 9 boys from the boys' school, the tutor began by discussing with the group the agenda for the session. It was decided to start off with a group discussion about the forthcoming residential trip, followed by a period of individual study.

The tutor facilitated the discussion and ensured that everyone participated. It transpired that two groups would be visiting a residential centre in Northumbria, one beginning at the beginning of August and the other at the end of August. Members of the group felt that as there were likely to be few black people where they were going their behaviour would be closely observed by local residents. Concern was expressed that if members of the first group misbehaved it would make it difficult for those who followed them. In particular, concern was expressed about some of the girls being allowed to participate in the expedition, as the group felt that some of them would not behave in an appropriate manner. This led to a thoughtful discussion about who should be invited. It was suggested that certain named individuals should only be invited if there was evidence of an improvement in their behaviour. The tutor said that she would put this recommendation to the girls' tutor.

While allowing the discussion to flow the tutor used the debate to reinforce some of the material that had been covered in earlier classes. There was an excellent rapport between the tutor and members of the group.

Following a short break, individuals either worked alone or in pairs on a number of different tasks, which included a spelling exercise and some basic arithmetic. A mentor joined the group at this stage and took an active part in the class.

The expedition to Northumbria was an integral part of several after-school classes. In addition to providing an opportunity for young people to work co-operatively in groups to plan all aspects of the expedition, it was an opportunity to develop more specific skills – maths, reading, writing. The young people had to calculate distances, allocate and manage budgets, write or telephone for information as well as keep a written log of activities and write letters home to family and mentors. Computing, word processing and graphical skills were used to create a record of the trip.

The case studies indicated the importance of identifying material and issues that the young people could engage with or relate to.

The accounts so far suggest that classes ran smoothly, but that was not always the case. Some classes were interrupted by inappropriate behaviour and while attempts were made to redeem the situation by discussion and negotiation, sometimes discipline had to be enforced and young people were sent home. Reflecting on her experience, one tutor said that what she had "learned from the young people is the importance of setting and keeping clear boundaries" and that the young people would rather that she were strict than friendly if it meant they knew where they stood.

Much of the work undertaken during the classes was displayed at presentation evenings and these provided important opportunities for parents to see what their child had been doing, the progress that he or she had made and to get feedback from the tutors. The young people also took pride in being able to present their work.

The continuity in staffing at the project in Year 3 facilitated closer interaction and co-operation with the schools. This led to other initiatives and a more flexible approach to the delivery of the education component. In particular, the tutors began holding one or two sessions in school. This entailed withdrawing individuals or a small number of pupils from class by prior arrangement and working on specific needs as identified earlier by the project in partnership with the young person and the school.

As already indicated, the education component was also built around other experiences such as the trips organised in the school holidays. In Year 1 two separate expeditions to Northumbria were arranged. In total 13 young people took part together with three mentors and two tutors. In Year 2 seven young people stayed in a youth hostel for two days in Hastings and one tutor took a small party to spend a day in a mock African village in Essex. In Year 3, 15 young people went on a four-day trip to North Norfolk to participate in environmental studies, walking and other outdoor pursuits. Two students were enrolled at the Hackney Summer University; one to study song writing, the other dance. In addition, a skeleton programme of classes was maintained at the DYP centre for those who had not gone away and wished to attend.

Following her appointment, the mentor co-ordinator started a Newsletter which was published seven or eight times a year (approximately monthly when the project was in 'full swing' between April and December). Each issue was four pages in length and in addition to recording essential dates when events were to take place, it was used as a vehicle for the young people to present their work and to reflect on their involvement in the project. Young people also took it in turns to assist with the production of the Newsletter. Mentors also contributed.

Young people's views of the after-school classes

The young people's views on the after-school classes were explored in interview. There was also an opportunity for the evaluators to talk informally with individuals as they worked in class. It was evident that, in the main, those present were enjoying the sessions and gaining something from them. As one young person said,

"I don't mind coming here... it can be hard at times ... but [the tutor] makes it fun. I like the short breaks... she makes us feel relaxed, I don't feel relaxed at school."

Another remarked:

"This is helping me with my maths...I know my six times table now."

The regular attenders in particular all claimed to enjoy the after-school sessions. For example, when asked what he liked best about the project, one young person replied without hesitation:

"The people that I meet and the work that I do ... we do maths, English and science .. things like that .. things to make your mind work .. it's harder than school but I like it."

Many commented upon the way they were taught:

"I like the maths, it's not like in school, not boring ... it's taught like a game."

"When [the tutor] teaches you she makes it fun; at school it's boring, she makes it good, exciting. You are enjoying yourself at the same time as learning."

Obviously these comments reflected the views of those who attended classes. Those who did not had different views. They said that they found the classes boring. Some said that the work was "too easy" whereas others said that there was "too much work". It was not always possible to gauge whether what the young people said was the true reason or a rationalisation for not attending classes.

Participation in the after-school classes

Detailed attendance records were not kept during Year 1 but it was possible to classify the 26 young people who started the project according to their participation in the educational classes. This is detailed below.

Never participated after the residential weekend	5	(3 boys, 2 girls)
Came once or twice to begin with or dropped in on a very irregular basis	6	(5 boys, 1 girl)
Good attenders at the beginning then left part way through	4	(3 boys, 1 girl)
Regular and committed attenders	11	(7 boys, 4 girl)

It could be seen that, at most, 15 young people (those falling into the last two categories) engaged with the educational programme in Year 1.

There did not appear to be any significant differences between the Year 8 and Year 9 boys in terms of their engagement with the project. The attendance of the girls fell sharply during the time the classes were held at Girls School. In fact only one girl was regularly attending. When the classes moved to the DYP premises three of the girls rejoined and attended regularly until the end of the project. (In part this vindicates the view formed by the project and the schools that the classes were more successful if held 'off-site'.) Registers were kept in Years 2 and 3 and more precise measures of attendance were available. The attendance of Cohort 2 is presented in Table 7.

Two features stand out. First, there was significant variation in attendance between young people. Two girls did not start the after-school classes and three Year 9 boys attended in the first term and were not seen again. Apart from the two girls who did not wish to take part, the other seven girls attended fairly regularly in the first two terms. However, at the end of the summer term they became disenchanted with the teacher and refused to come – bar one who continued to attend to the end, achieving an 88 per cent attendance. Despite this and because of their good attendance in the first two terms, four girls achieved more than 50 per cent attendance throughout the year. One boy also attended consistently achieving 71 per cent attendance. One other boy achieved over 50 per cent attendance.

Second, attendance declined over time and there was a step decline after each holiday break; from 54 per cent to 31 per cent to 18 per cent. The disruption of the holiday broke continuity and fewer returned after it. This is a familiar pattern at all evening classes – whatever the subject, academic level or age of the participants. This suggested that more needed to be done at the beginning of each term to 'kick start' the project so in Year 3 letters were written to each young person welcoming them back and tutors visited them and their parents in their homes in preparation for the new term.

Table 7: Attendance at education classes: Cohort 2

	Feb/Mar/ Apr	May/Jun/ Jul	Sep/Oct/ Nov	% attendance throughout year
Girls School				
Number of sessions	23	35	14	
Y8G1	19	19	0	53
Y8G2	20	31	12	88
Y8G3	21	19	6	64
Y8G4	12	12	2	36
Y8G5	18	10	3	43
Y8G6	23	19	0	58
Y8G7	20	18	1	54
Y8G8	0	0	0	0
Y8G9	0	0	0	0
Attendance for group	64%	41%	19%	
Boys School				
Number of sessions	30	28	18	
Y9				
Y9B1	12	4	0	21
Y9B2	22	11	9	55
Y9B3	19	24	11	71
Y9B4	18	6	0	32
Y9B5	8	2	0	13
Y9B6	9	0	0	12
Y9B7	3	0	0	4
Attendance for group	43%	24%	16%	
Number of sessions	24	31	21	
Y8				
Y8B1	18	4	12	45
Y8B2	14	9	0	30
Y8B3	14	9	2	33
Y8B4	17	5	0	29
Y8B5	14	6	5	33
Y8B6	16	18	3	49
Y8B7	12	2	10	32
Y8B8	7	12	0	25
Y8B9	10	6	0	21
Y8B10	6	6	6	24
Attendance for group	53%	25%	18%	
Attendance for all groups	54%	31%	18%	

Key: Y8G1, Year 8 Girl 1; Y9B1, Year 9 Boy 1; Y8B1, Year 8 Boy 1

Attendance in Year 3 is given in Table 8.

Table 8: Attendance at education classes: Cohort 3

	Mar/Apr/ May/Jun/Jul	Sep/Oct/ Nov	Jan/Feb	% attendance throughout year
Girls School				
Number of sessions	31	21	10	
Y8G1	31	20	6	92
Y8G2	30	21	1	84
Y8G3	0	0	0	0
Y8G4	29	21	10	97
Y8G5	26	19	8	85
Y8G6	26	19	10	89
Y8G7	22	21	0	68
Y8G8	Started Sept	19	10	95
Y8G9	19	19	9	76
Attendance for group	74%	84%	60%	
Boys School				
Number of sessions	32	16	9	
Y8B1	7 0	0	12	
Y8B2	4	2	3	16
Y8B3	15	5	4	42
Y8B4	17	8	5	53
Y8B5	19	14	8	72
Y8B6	13	2	0	26
Y8B7	12	13	9	60
Y8B8	19	8	6	58
Y8B9	10	4	0	25
Attendance for group	40%	39%	43%	
Mixed School				
Number of sessions	32	20	5	
Y8B1	18	4	4	46
Y8B2	10	0	0	18
Y8B3	31	19	2	91
Y8B4	13	3	0	28
Y8B5	9	10	0	33
Y8B6	24	5	0	51
Y8B7	24	16	2	74
Y8B8	25	19	3	82
Y8B9	11	1	0	21
Y8B10	22	14	1	65
Attendance for group	58%	46%	24%	
Attendance for all three groups	57%	57%	46%	

Key: Y8G1, Year 8 Girl 1; Y9B1, Year 9 Boy 1; Y8B1, Year 8 Boy 1

It can be seen that attendance did improve in Year 3 and was more consistent throughout the year. The steps the project had taken were working. Obviously the greater continuity of staffing played a part. Not only was this less disruptive to the young people but it also enabled closer and stronger links with the schools to be built up.

Reasons for 'dropping out' of the after-school classes

Following the concern at the decline in attendance in Year 2, all the young people were followed up to identify why they had been absent from classes. Interviews with the young people, project staff and school representatives revealed the following reasons why the young people stopped attending the after-school classes.

5   Did not drop out: were attending regularly at the end of the year.

3   Two girls did not want to attend the classes but wanted a mentor; One boy attended three times but was not interested in participating further.

4   Absented themselves from mainstream school and the school had no subsequent contact with them. They did not attend DYP either.

5   At the end of the summer term five girls left when relations broke down with the tutor.

9   This group gave a variety of reasons when interviewed – some more than one reason – and it was not always clear which reason was paramount and which was merely a rationalisation. The young people invariably said that the classes were "boring" or that others had left so they could not see "much point in going".They then said that the after school classes clashed with other activities, such as, swimming club, cadets, basketball, "jobs for mum and gran" and part-time job (helping uncle on stall).

6   **Parenting Component**

Despite early efforts, this component of the project turned out to be the most difficult to organise and the least successful. The project had aimed to involve parents/guardians to a great extent, provide bi-monthly parenting skills sessions and to make home visits in order to undertake family counselling where appropriate.

In Year 1 parents were contacted and provided with information about the project. Nearly one-half of the parents attended a joint parent mentor evening but enthusiasm soon evaporated afterwards. The first parenting session, which was to discuss schooling, attracted some parents, but plans for subsequent meetings were dropped when it became apparent that attendance would be very low. Half way through the first year of the project it was decided to change tack and tutors endeavoured to visit parents. The purpose of these visits was primarily to encourage parents to support their young persons' participation in the education component, not to offer any parenting skills training or family counselling.

Other initiatives were tried in subsequent years. In Year 2 a 'parent befriending programme' was implemented. The inspiration came from the CHANCE project in nearby Islington and involved a trained befriender being assigned to a parent to offer advice and support in much the same way that a mentor relates to his or her mentee. The scheme was not a success. Four parents showed initial interest but only one pairing was set up. As a result of this lack of interest, the scheme was not considered to be a priority for the third year of the project.

On reflection it appeared that most parents saw the project as being for the young people, not for them. Parents and guardians had to agree to their child being on the project and many (at least one-half) attended the initial meeting to hear about the project and to meet mentors and tutors. Invariably parents and family members of between six and ten young people attended presentation evenings and there was always a good turn out at Graduation Night, where a large number of parents attended to see their child receive his or her certificate. However, in the limited meetings that could be arranged between the evaluators and parents, it was apparent that parents were not prepared to give any additional time to the project themselves over and above that required to support their child. In many cases, parents' own lives were so disorganised or parents were under such extreme pressure coping on their own with other children that additional commitment was unrealistic.

After the initial setback, it was decided by the project – and endorsed by the steering committee – that the parenting component should involve tutors visiting the parents in their homes to 'increase the information flow between tutors and the home' and to encourage participation in the presentation evenings. Through this engagement, parents were consulted about other activities that might be arranged specifically for them. Project staff never ceased considering sessions for parents. A couple of sessions were run on English as an Additional Language and one on drug awareness. Parent support sessions were held in Year 3 and the project gave significant support to individual parents when their child was experiencing extreme difficulties. Examples included an occasion when one young person ran away from home, another when a young person was facing prosecution for a criminal offence and a further instance when relations between the school and the parents had broken down over the behaviour of their child. In each case, and as a result of the trust engendered, project staff (and the mentor in some cases) were able to provide essential advice and support or an important channel of communication between the parties concerned.

Towards the end of Year 3, DYP teamed up with Hackney Leisure and Learning to offer a six-week programme aimed primarily at young parents. The course was designed to explore ethnic and cultural roots, the parent-child relationship, self-esteem and self- discipline and how to access community resources. The programme was arranged to take place in May and June 2000, after the end of Year 3, and thus was outside the scope of this evaluation.

Some parents viewed the project as a 'treat' which could be denied their child as a sanction for misbehaviour. One parent withdrew her child from attending the residential weekend and one even prevented her son from attending Graduation Night and from receiving a certificate of commendation. At least one other young person was 'gated' for not returning home on time and prevented from attending the after-school classes for some considerable time.

Each project year formally ended with the Graduation Night at which young people and mentors received certificates of commendation for their efforts and performance. All three Graduation Nights observed followed a similar pattern and started with performances by the young people. These included a dance routine that a group of young people had devised and choreographed, a play that they had written about working and functioning as a class, and a drum recital.

The Mayor of Hackney attended the Graduation Night for Year 1. Two local black comedians (one of whom had been a pupil at the boys' school) presented the certificates in Years 1 and 2. In Year 3 this duty was performed by a prominent actor who had connections locally and was at the time appearing in the TV series *The Bill*. Each young person and mentor who graduated was photographed receiving their certificate, and group photographs were taken.

After the formal presentations food was prepared and served by the young people and the project staff. In Year 2 this was organised and supervised by one of the mentors who was a chef by training!

Each Graduation Night was fully supported by parents, family and friends. The main hall at the Round Chapel was packed on each occasion. About 100 people attended and everyone present obviously enjoyed the occasion. Representatives from the schools pointed out that these were young people who had not succeeded before at any academic endeavour, and it was very evident how much satisfaction, pride and self-esteem succeeding at DYP had given them.

Understandably the project wished to be as inclusive as possible and erred on the side of generosity in rewarding achievement. After the first Graduation Night some young people were unhappy that others who had not committed themselves fully to the project were nevertheless felt to have graduated. Their concerns were reported to the steering committee by the school representatives, and in subsequent years (Years 2 and 3) certificates recorded the specific contribution and commitment of the young person and a record of any progress made.

8   Impact of the Project

Previous sections have looked at participation in the project – in particular the extent to which mentoring relationships were formed and maintained throughout the year of the project and the extent to which young people participated in the education component. In addition, information had been presented on the numbers attending the residential weekend and other events and activities organised by the project. The involvement of parents has also been considered. In this section the success of the project is examined by assessing 'outputs' and the effect of the project on the young people.

Impact can be measured along various dimensions. Reflecting the aims of the project and what it set out to achieve, the five most important dimensions are the extent to which the project:

1. improved the young person's functioning in mainstream school;

2. improved literacy, numeracy and IT skills;

3. improved behaviour and social skills;

4. improved confidence and self-esteem; and

5. reduced the risk and incidence of offending.

A simple output measure is the number of young people graduating from the project each year who received a certificate of commendation in acknowledgement of their efforts. The number graduating each year is given in Table 9.

Table 9: Number of young people graduating from the project

	Year 1	Year 2	Year 3
Number of young people graduating	17	18	22

It can be seen that approximately two-thirds of young people graduated in Years 1 and 2 and a higher proportion, about three-quarters, graduated in Year 3.

Mere graduation, however, does not indicate the ways in which the project impacted on the young person. In Years 2 and 3 each certificate of commendation cited the specific achievements of each graduate. For the entire graduation group, 146 citations were made, on average 3.6 for each of the 40 graduates. Although there may have been a natural temptation to overstate achievement, there were good reasons for believing that the record on the certificate represented a reasonably accurate assessment of the impact of the project.

- Some citations, such as "good attendance at DYP" and "maintained contact with mentor", could be checked against formal records. Checking revealed close correspondence, and in the case of the mentoring relationship the number of citations was less than indicated by other records. Furthermore there were a few other instances where the number of citations under-recorded achievement.

- The assessments recorded on the certificates corresponded with the assessments given by project staff and school representatives independently to the evaluators.

- To reward effort project staff did not always feel obliged to record improvements. A good number of citations were in recognition of contributions made or of activities undertaken. Examples include:

"Has co-operated with other students at DYP".

"Co-operates well in the classroom".

"Took great care of the DYP garden".

"Co-operative member of residential and trips".

"Interest in news and current affairs".

"Active participation in presentation evenings".

While citations provided a starting-point, they were cross-checked with project staff and school representatives. Any errors were corrected and omissions added, but this process led to few changes to the initial record. How the project impacted on the young people is given in Table 10.

Table 10: The impact of the project: Years 2 and 3*

	Year 2	Year 3
Improved functioning at school		
Improved school attendance	4	1
Improved school work	2	2
Improved behaviour at school	3	6
Improved literacy, numeracy and IT skills	11	11
Improved behaviour and social skills	11	12
Improved confidence and/or self-esteem	10	10
Number of young people showing		
any of the above improvements	16	16

* No citations were given in Year 1.

It can be seen from Table 10 that between 10 and 12 young people had improved their behaviour, self-esteem and academic competencies. To some extent these three aspects go 'hand in hand'. The young people came from disadvantaged home backgrounds, they lacked confidence and self-esteem, had become disruptive and were not succeeding in mainstream school. A mutually reinforcing downward spiral had set in, and to reverse that decline all three aspects had to be addressed. Certainly early in the project the tutors' priority was to address behaviour, to establish rapport and to teach the young people how to function in a classroom environment. Much time was spent addressing behavioural problems and trying to encourage the young people to reflect on their aggressive or disruptive behaviour and to 'settle' as a group. At the same time the tutors sought to instil an interest in learning and to give the young people greater self-esteem and confidence to achieve academically. At that point they could move on to address specific skills.

The importance of addressing attitudes towards education was recognised by one mother talking about her son on DYP.

"[He] *now seems to understand that school is important and he believes in himself.*"

Mentors too played a part in improving behaviour, in raising self-esteem and in reinforcing the messages from other parts of the programme. Comments like the following were frequently encountered in interviews.

"*I think* [mentee's name] *is now less quick to lose his temper. He's able to talk about how he feels. This has helped him a lot. He now gets on better with his mum and he is not fighting as much.*"

The contribution of the mentor was acknowledged by a parent.

"Having a mentor has been so good for him. She has had the time to discuss things with him and listen to him. She even got him doing subjects that he wouldn't do before. She takes him to the library to study in peace and quiet."

Their ability to function as a group was evident at presentation evenings and Graduation Night. In Year 3, when the girls prepared and performed a play about their experiences at DYP, the school representative was prompted to remark:

"I didn't believe that they could co-operate to organise such an event."

Formal verification of any improvements in educational attainment was possible in Year 3 when the project administered reading and mathematics tests. These were nationally recognised tests currently being used by the LEA for young people of low educational standard. In total 19 young people took the initial test shortly after joining the project in spring 1999 and 13 took the follow-up test one year later, in spring 2000, towards the end of the project year. However, only nine took the tests on both occasions and could be included in any 'before and after' comparison. Their results are set out in Table 11.

Table 11: Literacy and numeracy 'before and after' test results

	Reading test (Max. score 48)		Maths test 1 (Max. score 26)		Maths test 2 (Max. score 41)	
	Before	After	Before	After	Before	After
Boy 1	42	44	21	18	21	-
Boy 2	44	42	22	21	40	39
Boy 3	40	39	19	19	-	21
Boy 4	44	47	24	26	34	35
Boy 5	41	43	21	25	6	-
Girl 1	36	38	20	26	21	25
Girl 2	31	34	17	22	9	-
Girl 3	38	45	16	21	10	11
Girl 4	27	30	17	20	-	2

It can be seen from Table 11 that six of the nine (boys 4 and 5 and all the girls) showed some improvement during the year. The results were not spectacular and the project tutors did not claim them to be. For the tutors, any improvement in educational attainment was confirmation that their main objective of helping the young people to better 'cope' with schooling had been achieved.

Progress at DYP was not always matched by progress at school. Only a small number had shown improvements in school attendance, school work or behaviour at school (see Table 10). There are two obvious reasons for this disparity. First, any improvements at the project were so small to be imperceptible in the setting of mainstream school. Second, while the young people may have engaged positively with the project, their attitude to mainstream school and their ability to function in it had not been affected. Nevertheless, while dramatic changes were not evident to the school, for some progress had been made. School representatives would comment: "at least you could talk to [young person] now", indicating that now disruptive behaviour could at least be addressed.

For at least three people the school felt that the project had made them worse. These were young people who constantly sought attention and they had exploited the opportunity that the project had presented to gain yet more attention.

Longer-term outcomes

At the end of Year 3 schools were asked to assess the subsequent progress of those 52 young people who had been included in the project in the first two years. Were they still attending school or had they dropped out or been excluded? Were they truanting or causing disruption, or had their behaviour improved? Many had left the school and were said to be 'off roll'. This could have occurred at any time for a variety of reasons. It was noted earlier that some left during the course of the project, which was their reason for not participating further, and others moved from the area shortly after the end of the project. Some simply wished to transfer to a different school. Twelve young people fell into this category and could not be followed up. Schools provided follow- up information on the remaining 40.

According to the information provided by the schools, the 40 young people were categorised as either a 'success' or a 'failure'. Those who had dropped out, were frequently truanting or were very disruptive were classified as failures. Success was the absence of these adverse indicators. The young people in the first year of the project had now reached school leaving age (the Year 9 group) or were about to (the Year 8 group). A positive indicator of success for them was whether they had completed school and had been entered for GCSEs.

Of the 40 young people 19 were judged to have been a success and 21 a failure. In order to assess whether the project had contributed to a young person's success the group was divided according to whether they had participated in the project. In the first instance participation was taken to be that the young person had been a regular and committed attendee of the educational classes. The outcomes are shown in Table 12.

Table 12: Longer-term success by participation in the educational classes

| | Regular and committed attendee of educational classes | | Not regular and committed attendee of educational classes | | Total |
	Number	Per cent	Number	Per cent	
Success	17	89	6	23	23
Failure	2	11	20	77	22
Total	19	100	26	100	45

It can be seen that those who took full part in the educational classes at the project were much more likely to be a success in the longer term. A full 87 per cent of those who participated in the educational classes were judged to have been a success compared with only 24 per cent of those who did not participate. This relationship was found to be statistically significant (Chi-square 22.0, 1df, p < 0 .001). Although this is encouraging, it should be remembered that those not attending the project are not a true control group but merely those who were initially selected for the project but chose not to continue after the early stages. Thus the results may simply reflect a 'selection effect' – that is, those who continued with the project were the better prospects of success regardless of the achievements of the project.

A similar analysis could be undertaken for the mentoring component of the project. This time young people were differentiated according to whether they had a good relationship with their mentor. The results are shown in Table 13.

Table 13: Longer-term success by relationship with mentor

	Good relationship with mentor		Not good relationship with mentor		Total
	Number	Per cent	Number	Per cent	
Success	12	57	11	46	23
Failure	9	43	13	55	22
Total	21	100	24	100	45

It can be seen from Table 13 that those having a mentor were more likely to be successful in the longer term. However, this association was not so marked and did not attain statistical significance.

Offending behaviour

The final criterion on which the project could be assessed was its aim to reduce the risk of offending. From the Police National Computer database the local police identified all cautions and convictions at court recorded against the 80 young people on the project.

It was noted earlier that eight young people had been cautioned or convicted of an offence before joining the project. Fifteen committed offences during the time that they were assigned to the project (whether or not they participated) and 17 offended after they had left the project. As some offenders committed offences in more than one period the figures overstate the number of young people involved in crime. Of the 80 young people 32 (40%) were cautioned or convicted of an offence at some stage. There was a difference between boys and girls; only three of the 26 girls (12%) committed offences compared with 29 of the 54 boys (54%). It is difficult to set these figures in context as the young people were all at different ages (between 13 and 17) at the time they were followed up and some had been followed up for two years whereas Cohort 3 had only just left the project. Nevertheless, by any comparison a significant number of boys were involved in crime.

Details of the types of crime committed are shown in Table 14.

Table 14: Number and type of offences committed by the young people

Type of offence	Before joining project	During project	After leaving project	Total
Violence	1	2	7	10
Robbery	2	1	5	8
Burglary	-	2	2	4
Theft and handling-	-	3	7	10
Shoplifting	2	6	4	12
Theft of motor vehicle/TADA	1	2	2	5
Theft from motor vehicle	-	-	2	2
Interfering with a motor vehicle	-	3	1	4
Criminal damage	1	2	2	5
Drugs	-	-	2	2
Possession of weapon	-	1	3	4
Disorderly behaviour	-	-	1	1
Motoring offences	1	-	5	6
Failing to surrender to bail	-	-	1	1
Number of offences	8	22	44	74
Number of offenders	8	15	17	32*

*32 different young people committed crime at some point.

It can be seen from Table 14 that the young people committed a wide variety of offences before during and after being on the project. The majority were property offences but there were also some serious crimes against the person. Of the 10 offences of violence, two were grievous bodily harm (GBH) and four actual bodily harm (ABH).

As in all analyses of criminal careers (Tarling, 1993) some offenders commit few offences whereas others commit many. About one-half (15) of the young people who had committed offences had only committed one offence. At the other extreme, two young people had committed six offences and one seven offences.

In order to assess whether participation in the project reduced subsequent involvement in crime further comparative analysis was undertaken. The analysis was confined to the boys in Years 1 and 2. The results are shown in Table 15.

Table 15: Offending during the follow up period by participation in the educational classes

During follow-up period	Regular and committed attendee of educational classes		Not regular and committed attendee of educational classes		Total
	Number	Per cent	Number	Per cent	
Not offended	8	73	13	54	21
Offended	3	27	11	46	14
Total	11	100	24	100	35

It can be seen that those who participated in the project were less likely to offend during the follow-up period than those who did not participate. However, the number on which this is based is small and the association did not reach statistical significance.

The analysis was repeated according to whether or not the boy had a good relationship with his mentor. However, there appeared to be little association between whether a good mentoring relationship had been formed and whether or not the boy subsequently committed an offence.

9 Conclusions

The DYP II was initiated to work with vulnerable young people at a formative stage in their lives. Early adolescence is a time when young people who are experiencing difficulties in achieving academically can turn their back on school. It is also a time when they may develop deviant lifestyles including involvement in crime. The selection criteria adopted by the project ensured that those young people who were referred to the project and selected for it were certainly 'at risk' of such outcomes. They were not succeeding at school, they were exhibiting behavioural problems and they were showing early signs of becoming delinquent. On paper they were a challenging group, and everyone who came into contact with them found them to be a challenging group. It is within this context and against that background that the project should be judged.

Project implementation

The project planned to work with 30 young people each year. But this figure was never achieved. Over the three year period 80 young people were selected for the project – 10 short of the target. It was felt that the shortfall was due to the severe and rigid selection criteria – not enough young people met the necessary conditions to be considered. (There was also the view – discussed later – that the criteria identified unsuitable young people.) As a result the project relaxed the criteria which in later years came to be used as selection guidelines rather than conditions which had to be strictly adhered to. By Year 3 the project had adopted a policy of selecting more than the required number of young people – keeping one or two on a reserve list should any of those selected drop out. This helped in Year 3 (which achieved the highest number of referrals –28) when two reserves joined the project at a later date. However, this policy could only be implemented early in the project cycle as there was little to be gained by young people joining the project late in the cycle.

Retaining young people who did join was hard. The project faced a difficult task in trying to deliver in effect extra schooling to a group whose only defining characteristic was that they were disenchanted with school. Perhaps not surprisingly some young people ceased to engage with the project shortly after the start. Project staff worked hard to keep young people on the project and developed strategies throughout the three-year period to keep attrition rates low. They visited parents and young people in their homes, wrote letters at crucial times throughout the year and went in to schools to make contact with the young people.

Maintaining contact during school holidays was important and this was achieved by organising activities and expeditions and by running a 'skeleton' time-table of classes.

Retention of staff was equally difficult and equally important. It was no surprise that Year 3 ran more smoothly and effectively as a result of the continuity of staffing throughout the year.

Over time, and drawing on the lessons learned, the project came to be better organised and more professionally administered. Contacts with young people, parents, schools and mentors became more frequent and more systematic. Formal records of attendance were kept, individual education plans were introduced and more formal feedback in the form of written reports was prepared. However, to succeed in engaging the young people, the project had to be careful not to be so formally structured and organised as to be seen by the young people themselves as simply another school. Engendering a sense of 'ownership' of the project and a feeling that the centre was 'their' space, was important but meant that things did not always go according to plan.

The project did not only consist of after-school classes. A key feature was the mentoring component – each young person was matched with an adult mentor. During the three- year period the project was able to recruit sufficient mentors but signs were emerging that this was becoming more difficult. DYP now faces intense competition from other projects and posts for mentors are also being created within statutory agencies such as schools. Although DYP had run a mentoring project prior to the start of this project, some initial problems emerged. The project responded by appointing a part-time mentoring co-ordinator and provided on-going help through mentoring support evenings. The mentoring co-ordinator was also able to do much by way of prompting and facilitating contact between mentors and mentees. About one-half of the mentoring relationships lasted the 12-month period.

The initial aims of the parenting component were not fully achieved. It became clear early on that parents saw the project as being for their son or daughter, not for themselves. Parents, guardians and family members did attend presentation evenings and Graduation Night, events to celebrate their child's achievements, but they did not sign up in large numbers to activities specifically designed to develop their own parenting skills.

The residential weekend got the project off to a memorable start and helped in establishing contact between staff, young people and mentors.

Project impact

The initial application for funding, prepared by Crime Concern, claimed that the project would lead to 'short term benefits (over the course of one year) including: 75% of participants will demonstrate improved school attendance; 75% of participants will demonstrate improved academic performance; 70% of participants will not offend/reoffend'. Clearly these expectations were not realistic.

The project undoubtedly had some success, and a comparison between those who participated and those who did not would seem to support this. The project's impact on offending behaviour, however, was disappointing. Up to one-half of those attending derived benefit from the project. Although the results from the measurable outcomes did not show substantial improvement, there were observable changes in behaviour and attitudes to learning. Gains were often modest and a comment frequently made was: "you can at least talk to him (or her) now". These young people could reflect a little more on their own behaviour and see another person's point of view.

The project had a significant impact on a few. Everyone associated agreed that in the case of five or six young people the project 'turned them round'. The project inspired these young people and raised their self-esteem. Examining the circumstances of these particular young people it was difficult to identify any common factor, either in terms of their characteristics or the specific element of the project that triggered the change. It just seemed that the project came at the right time in their lives. A mentor (a new and influential person) opened up fresh horizons or helped by simply 'talking things through'. The educational classes also gave them confidence and a sense that they could achieve.

The gains at the project were not always transferred to school. However, the schools fully recognised the challenges that the young people presented and the poor prognosis of their staying in school. The project, they said had helped to 'hold on' to the young person for another year. Several commentators associated with the project felt that one year was not sufficient. It had taken a year to build a relationship with the young person and to establish trust. By the end of the year the young people were just 'learning how to learn', to settle and to function in class. They felt that those who had participated, and were beginning to turn the corner, should be kept on the project longer in order to make the necessary further progress. If this project could not do it then some other project should be in place to do so. In this context it was interesting to note that six of the young people in Cohort 1 who were considered to have successfully completed school were subjected to other intensive projects run by the school. This suggests that sustained intervention is needed. A project such as DYP on its own can be expected to make only a limited contribution in one year.

About one-half of the people recruited to the project left early and gained little from the project. Those that could be followed up failed in the sense that their behaviour did not improve and, in some cases, deteriorated. They were frequently absent from school and some had virtually dropped out. The fact that the project could not even begin to address the needs of so many, raises issues about the kinds of young people the project should be trying to reach. It was said of one class and of other individuals that they 'were too far gone' before the project intervened and that 'the cause had already been lost'. Some felt that the strict referral criteria inevitably brought on to the project unsuitable young people for whom this kind of intervention was inappropriate. The project has to strike a difficult and delicate balance. On the one hand the project exists to help those at risk, but it does not want to be expending its resources unnecessarily on those it cannot help, especially when those resources could be better directed at those it could help.

References

Audit Commission (1996) *Misspent Youth*, London: HMSO.

Clarke, A. (1999). *Evaluation Research*, London: Sage.

Clawson, J. G. (1980) 'Mentoring in managerial careers', in C. B. Derr (Ed.), *Work, Family and the Career: New Frontiers in Theory and Research*, New York: Praeger, pp. 144-165.

Collins, E. G. C. and Scott, P. (1978) 'Everybody who makes it has a mentor', *Harvard Business Review*, July/August, pp. 89-102.

Collins, P. (1993) 'The interpersonal vicissitudes of mentorship: an exploratory study of the field supervisor-student relationship', *The Clinical Supervisor*, 11 (1): 121-135.

Dondero, G. M. (1997) 'Mentors: beacons of hope', *Adolescence*, 32 (128): 881-86.

Farrington, D. (1996) *Understanding and Preventing Youth Crime*, York: Joseph Rowntree Foundation.

Freedman, M. (1993) *The Kindness of Strangers: Adult Mentors, Urban Youth and the New Voluntarism*, New York: Josey Bass.

Gottlieb, B. and Sylvestre, J. C. (1994), Social support in the relationship between older adolescents and adults, in F. Nestmann and K. Hurrelmann (eds) *Social Networks and Social Support in Childhood and Adolescence*, New York: de Gruyter.

Graham, J. and Bowling, B. (1995) *Young People and Crime*, London: Home Office.

Griffiths, S. (1996) *The Challenge: A Profile of Poverty in Hackney*. London: The London Borough of Hackney.

Hamilton, S. F. (ed) (1991) *Unrelated Adults in Adolescent Lives*, Occasional Paper No. 29, New York: Cornell University.

Hamilton, S. F. and Darling, N. (1989) 'Mentors in adolescent lives', in K. Hurrelmann and U. Engel (eds) *The Social World of Adolescents*, New York: de Gruyter.

Hernandez-Piloto Brito, H. (1992) 'Nurses in action: an innovative approach to mentoring', *Journal of Nursing Administration*, 22 (5): 23-8.

Home Office (1997) *No More Excuses: The New Approach to Tackling Youth Crime in England and Wales*, London: The Stationery Office.

Kram, K. E. (1985) *Mentoring at Work*, Glenville, IL: Scott Foresman.

Levinson, D. J., Darrow, C. N., Klein, E. B., Levinson, M. H. and McKee, B. (1978) *The Seasons of a Man's Life*, New York: Knopf.

National Mentoring Partnership http://www.mentoring.org/mentoring.html

McIntyre, D., Hagger, H. and Wilkin, M. (1993) *Mentoring: Perspectives on School-Based Teacher Education*, London: Kogan Page.

Morrow, K. V. and Styles, M. B. (1995) *Building Relationships with Youth in Program Settings: A Study of Big Brothers/Big Sisters*, Philadelphia: Public/Private Ventures.

Morton-Cooper, A. and Palmer, A. (1993) *Mentoring and Preceptorship: A Guide to Support Roles in Clinical Practice*, Oxford: Blackwell.

Philip, K. and Hendry, L. B. (1996) 'Young people and mentoring – towards a typology?' *Journal of Adolescence*, 19, 189-201.

Philip, K. and Hendry, L. B. (2000) 'Making sense of mentoring or mentoring making sense? Reflections on the mentoring process by adult mentors with young people', *Journal of Community and Applied Social Psychology*, 10, 211-223.

Porteous, D. (1998) *Evaluation of the CSV On-Line Mentoring Scheme*, Vauxhall Centre for the Study of Crime, University of Luton.

Rhodes, J., Ebert, L. and Fischer, K. (1992) 'Natural mentors: an overlooked resource in the social networks of adolescent mothers', *American Journal of Community Psychology*, 20 (4): 445-61.

Roberts, I. St J and Singh, C. S. (1999) *Using Mentors to Change Problem Behaviour in Primary School Children*, Research Findings No. 95, Research, Development and Statistics Directorate, London: Home Office.

Taibbi, R. (1983) 'Supervisors as mentors', *Social Work*, 28 (3): 237-38.

Tarling, R. (1993). *Analysing Offending*. London: HMSO.

Tierney, J. P. and Branch, A. Y. (1992) *College Students as Mentors for At-Risk Youth: A Study of Six Campus Partners in Learning Programs*, Philadelphia: Public/Private Ventures.

Tierney, J. P., Grossman, J. B. and Resch, N. L. (1995) *Making a Difference: An Impact Study of Big Brothers/Big Sisters*, Philadelphia: Public/Private Ventures.

RDS Publications

Requests for Publications

Copies of our publications and a list of those currently available may be obtained from:

> Home Office
> Research, Development and Statistics Directorate
> Communication Development Unit
> Room 275, Home Office
> 50 Queen Anne's Gate
> London SW1H 9AT
> Telephone: 020 7273 2084 (answerphone outside of office hours)
> Facsimile: 020 7222 0211
> E-mail: publications.rds@homeoffice.gsi.gov.uk

alternatively

why not visit the RDS website at
>   Internet: http://www.homeoffice.gov.uk/rds/index.html

where many of our publications are available to be read on screen or downloaded for printing.